REPLACEMENTS AND UPGRADES

Better Homes and Gardens® Plumbing
Editor: Larry Johnston
Copy Chief: Terri Fredrickson
Copy Editor: Kevin Cox
Publishing Operations Manager: Karen Schirm
Senior Editor, Asset & Information Management: Phillip Morgan
Edit and Design Production Coordinator: Mary Lee Gavin
Editorial and Design Assistant: Renee E. McAtee
Book Production Managers: Pam Kvitne, Marjorie J. Schenkelberg, Rick von Holdt, Mark Weaver
Imaging Center Operator: Patricia J. Savage
Contributing Copy Editor: Andrea Kline
Contributing Proofreaders: Pam Elizian, Sara Henderson, Willa Speiser
Contributing Technical Proofreader: Barbara L. Klein
Contributing Indexer: Don Glassman
Other Contributors: Janet Anderson

Additional Editorial Contributions from Abramowitz Creative Studios
Publishing Director/Designer: Tim Abramowitz
Designer/Illustrator: Kelly Bailey
Designer: Joel Wires
Photography: Image Studios
  Account Executive: Lisa Egan
  Photographer: Bill Rein
  Assistant: Rick Nadke

Meredith® Books
Editor in Chief: Gregory H. Kayko
Executive Director, Design: Matt Strelecki
Managing Editor: Amy Tincher-Durik
Executive Editor/Group Manager: Benjamin W. Allen
Senior Associate Design Director: Tom Wegner
Marketing Product Manager: Brent Wiersma

Editorial Director: Linda Raglan Cunningham
Executive Director, Marketing: Kevin Kacere
Executive Director, New Business Development: Todd M. Davis
Executive Director, Sales: Ken Zagor
Director, Operations: George A. Susral
Director, Production: Douglas M. Johnston
Director, Marketing & Publicity: Amy Nichols
Business Director: Jim Leonard

Vice President and General Manager: Douglas J. Guendel

Meredith Publishing Group
President: Jack Griffin
Senior Vice President: Karla Jeffries

Meredith Corporation
Chairman of the Board: William T. Kerr
President and Chief Executive Officer: Stephen M. Lacy

In Memoriam: E. T. Meredith III (1933–2003)

Better Homes and Gardens®

Plumbing

Meredith® Books
Des Moines, Iowa

Table of contents

SYSTEMS

TROUBLESHOOTING AND REPAIRS

TOOLS, MATERIALS, AND SKILLS

Systems

Getting to know your system

With so many pipes and fittings behind walls and under floors, a plumbing system seems complicated and mysterious to the inexperienced. But plumbing is actually a straightforward matter of distributing clean, incoming water to where it's wanted and facilitating the outflow of waste. Here's an overview of how household plumbing works.

Supply, drain, and vent systems

The supply system brings water into your house, divides it into hot and cold water lines, and distributes it to various fixtures (sinks, toilets, showers, tubs) and appliances (washing machines, dishwashers, water heaters, heating system boilers).

The drain system carries water away from the fixtures and appliances and out of the house.

The vent system supplies air to the drainpipes so waste flows out freely. Because drains and vents use the same types of pipes and are tied together, they often are referred to as the drain-waste-vent system (DWV).

Locating the water meter and main shutoffs

The first step toward mastering your house's plumbing system is to locate the water meter and the main shutoff.

Look for the place where the water supply enters your house. In most cases a pipe an inch or so thick, called a water main, comes up through the floor in the basement or on the first floor. If you have metered water, the pipe enters and exits a round gauge, the water meter, which has either a digital readout that looks like a car's odometer or a series of five or six dials. The meter records how much water passes into the house. If you have a well, or if your bill stays the same no matter how much water you use, you don't have a meter.

Near the place where the water main enters your house, you'll find one or two valves that you can turn on and off by hand. This is the main shutoff for the house.

An additional shutoff may be located outside the house buried in a compartment sometimes called a buffalo box. To find it, look for a round metal cover in the ground near the street or the edge of your property. (It may be overgrown with grass.)

Pry up the cover and look inside with a flashlight. There you'll find a valve that you can turn by hand or one that requires a special long-handled key. Older homes in warm-weather locations sometimes have an exposed valve just outside the house.

If you have an older home, don't depend entirely on the inside shutoff; it can break, leak, or fail completely. If you need to shut down the system often during a project, learn where the outside shutoff is and use it to shut off the water.

CAUTION

KNOW HOW TO SHUT OFF THE WATER

In case of a burst pipe or other emergency, be ready to shut off the main water supply quickly. Show members of your family where the main shutoff is. Clear away boxes and furniture so it is easy to reach. If it takes a special tool to shut off your water, keep that tool handy.

WHERE YOUR RESPONSIBILITY ENDS

The water meter is the Continental Divide for assigning responsibility for plumbing repairs. The water meter and pipes leading away from the house are the responsibility of the water company, and the water company should fix them for free. Anything on the house side of the meter is the homeowner's responsibility. However, if you plan to add new fixtures (not just replace old ones), your municipality might require that a larger water main come into the house. If so, you'll have to pay for it. Check when you get your permit.

THE NEW AND THE OLD

Years ago plumbers installed cast-iron drain lines. They packed each joint with tarred oakum, then poured in molten lead—a practice that dates back to the ancient Romans. For supply lines and smaller drain lines, they used galvanized pipe, which is strong but rusts and corrodes over time.

Plastic drain lines and copper supply lines have largely replaced the old materials. They last much longer and are easier to handle. However, it took years for different localities to make the switch to modern materials. In some places, for instance, building codes required cast iron into the 1980s, and today some municipalities still require galvanized pipe for water supply lines.

If your home has old pipe, there's no need to rip it out. Many products are available that make it easy to connect new materials to the old. Always check local codes to see what materials and fittings are required for health and safety.

The supply system

Water enters your house through a pipe that connects to either a municipal water line or a private well. If your bill changes according to how much water you use, your water flows through a water meter. Near the meter you will find one or two main shutoffs.

From there, water travels to the water heater. Water from a private well goes to a pressure tank before going to the heater.

From the water heater, a pair of water lines—one hot and one cold—branch out through the house to serve the various fixtures (toilets, tubs, sinks, showers) and water-using appliances (dishwashers, washing machines, heating system boilers).

These supply lines are always under pressure; if one is opened or a break occurs, water will shoot out until it is shut off in some way. That is why modern homes have stop (or shutoff) valves for every fixture and appliance. If your home is not equipped with stop valves, plan to install them. They make maintenance and repairs more convenient and more than pay for themselves should a serious break in the system occur.

Older homes have plumbing systems that use galvanized pipe, which corrodes over time, leading to low water pressure and leaks. The builders of newer homes use copper supply lines, and in some places plastic lines, both of which last much longer.

Bathroom sink (lavatory)

Stop (shutoff) valve

Main shutoff

Water meter

Water heater

Hot water supply

Cold water supply

Kitchen sink

Washing machine

Sill cock (faucet for garden hose)

SUPPLY SYSTEM PROBLEM SOLVER	
For answers to these problems and questions	**See pages**
Burst or leaking pipes	56–57
Installing stop valves	90
Installing new supply lines	128
Noisy pipes	88
Preventing frozen pipes	58–59
Removing and installing pipes and fittings	72–86
Repairing faucets	15–29, 92–95
Types, sizes of pipes and fittings	66–71
Water filters	110, 114
Water heaters	40–45, 98–101

The drain system

The drain system uses gravity to rid the house of liquid and solid waste. It also guards against foul-smelling and potentially harmful gases entering the house from the municipal drain system or the septic field.

All fixtures, with the exception of the toilet, empty into a trap (toilets have built-in traps). A trap is a curved section of drainpipe that holds enough standing water to make an airtight seal. The seal prevents sewer gases from backing up and leaking into the home. Each time a fixture is used, the old water in the trap is forced down the line and replaced with new water.

After leaving the trap, drain water travels through pipes sloped at no less than $1/4$ inch per foot toward a large, vertical pipe (called a waste stack or a soil pipe) that carries water below the floor. There it takes a bend and proceeds out to a municipal sewer line or a private septic system. A cleanout provides a place where you can insert an auger to clear the line. Traps serve the same function.

Drainpipes come in various diameters, depending on what they will be used for: $1\frac{1}{4}$-inch pipe for bathroom sinks, $1\frac{1}{2}$-inch for kitchen sinks and bathtubs, and 3- or 4-inch for toilets. The stack is usually a 4-inch pipe. Older homes use cast-iron pipe for the stacks and galvanized pipe for other drain lines. New homes use plastic, and occasionally copper, for stacks and drains.

Toilet with internal trap

Trap

Trap

Trap

Cleanout

Floor drain

Waste stack (soil pipe)

Flexible drain line for washing machine

DRAIN SYSTEM PROBLEM SOLVER

For answers to these problems and questions	See pages
Adding a plastic drain line	124
Clogged drains	46–55
Drain assemblies	60
New garbage disposer	102–103
Planning new drain lines	115
Tapping into drain lines	122–123
Toilets	36–39, 96–97
Tapping into a cast-iron drain line	125
Types of pipes and fittings	66–71
Working with plastic pipe and tubing	82–85

The vent system

To flow freely, drainpipes need air. Without air, water glugs down a drain like soda from a bottle. A plumbing vent plays the same role as the second, smaller opening in a gasoline can. With the opening closed, gas pours out slowly. But once the stopper is removed, air enters the can and allows the liquid to flow freely.

The air supplied by a vent also prevents siphoning action, which might otherwise pull water out of traps and toilets and allow sewage gases to enter the house. Instead, vents carry the gases through the roof. Sewer gas, composed largely of methane, is not only smelly, it is also harmful and dangerous. Don't be tempted to install a substandard venting system, even if it means avoiding a lot of work.

A main vent is an extension of the waste stack and reaches upward through the roof. Branch vents tie into the main vent. Every plumbing fixture and appliance must be vented properly, either tying into a main vent or having a vent of its own that extends through the roof.

When installing a new fixture in a new location (not just replacing an existing fixture), venting is often the most difficult problem to overcome. Local codes require that venting meets specific dimension requirements. Research these requirements before you begin planning. Vent pipes are made of the same materials as drainpipes, though sometimes they are smaller in diameter.

VENT SYSTEM PROBLEM SOLVER	
For answers to these problems and questions	**See pages**
Adding a new vent	126–127
Fitting for vents	126–127
Planning drains and vents	115–117
Roof flashing for a vent	127
Tapping new vents into old	122–123
Tying a new plastic vent into a cast-iron vent	125
Types of pipe used for venting	66–67
Wet venting	116
Working with plastic pipe	82–85

Permits and codes

Working to code

You may be an amateur working on your own house, but you have the same responsibilities as a licensed plumber. The plumbing elements you repair or install must provide a supply of pure and wholesome water and must facilitate the safe passage of liquids, solid wastes, and gases out of your house. This means that you must use only those techniques and materials that are acceptable under the building codes in your area.

The procedures in this book represent the editors' understanding of the Uniform Plumbing Code (UPC). Local codes are based on this uniform code but can vary greatly. If no local codes cover the work you will be doing, consult the national codes. You'll find the latest edition of the UPC in the reference section of the library. If local codes do cover your project, they supersede any national requirements. (Canadian residents can obtain a copy of the Canadian Plumbing Code by contacting Publications Sales M-20, National Research Council of Canada, Ottawa, K1A 0R6 Ontario.)

Working with your local building department

Consult with your local building department if you plan to add or change your plumbing in any substantial way or if you believe the existing plumbing might be substandard. Plumbing codes may seem bothersome, but they are designed to make your home's plumbing system safe and worry-free. Those who ignore codes often make costly mistakes, create health hazards, and can have difficulty selling their homes later on.

If you will be adding new service—not just replacing one fixture with another one—check with your building department before proceeding. Neglecting to do so could cost you the expense and trouble of tearing out and redoing your work.

The inspector who comes to your house may be helpful, friendly, and flexible, or a real stickler. But no matter what, your job will proceed more smoothly if you follow these guidelines:

- To avoid asking unnecessary questions, find out as much pertinent information as possible about your project before you talk to an inspector. Your building department may offer literature concerning your type of installation. If not, consult national codes.
- Go to your inspector with a plan to be approved or amended; don't expect the building department to plan the job for you.
- Present your plan with neatly drawn diagrams and a complete list of the materials you will use.
- Be sure you clearly understand when you need to have inspections. Do not cover up any work that needs to be inspected.
- Be as courteous as possible. Inspectors are often wary of homeowners because so many are ignorant of codes and procedures. Show the inspector you are serious about doing things the right way and comply with any requirements without argument.

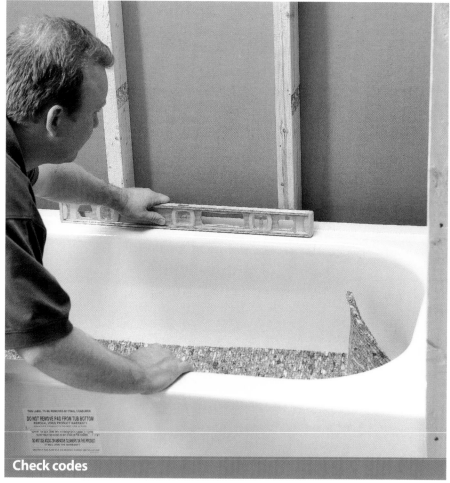

Check codes

Installing a tub or whirlpool is not a task you want to immediately redo to fix a code violation. Check local building codes before you begin a plumbing project to ensure you proceed according to code the first time.

Mapping your system

The plumbing in households remains hidden, for the most part, behind floors, walls, and cabinets. If you venture into the unfinished portion of the basement or the part of the house that contains the heating system and water heater, you'll possibly see runs of copper water supply pipe or a drain stack made of PVC or cast iron. You may have even seen the small vent stacks of the drain-waste-vent system on the roof. Most people don't notice the plumbing system, except when there's a problem. Then it becomes a mysterious nuisance.

Before attempting a project, know and understand your plumbing system. If you are fortunate to have a blueprint of the plumbing drawings of your house, you can easily follow, understand, and know the location of piping, venting, and fixtures in your home. Though some plumbers stray from their plans slightly, the blueprint should be accurate. Make additional copies and mark the corrections as you find them on the copy. Also use the copies to plan and record modifications and additions to the plumbing system. If you don't have a blueprint of the plumbing system, grab graph paper, clipboard, scale, straightedge, and pencil to create your own.

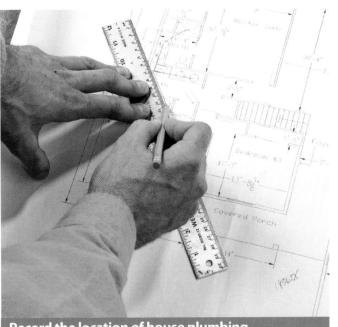

Record the location of house plumbing

Having an accurate drawing will make responding to an emergency easier as well as simplify remodeling of or additions to the system. To follow the route of a pipe, start where the main supply line enters the home. Continue to map the pipe to where it connects to the water heater. At that point, the pipe will exit the water heater with hot and cold lines. Mark the locations where these pipes branch off toward fixtures throughout the house. Remember that supply pipes must end near a drainpipe. When mapping the drainpipe system, work backward for the fixtures, mapping as you go.

You may find an access panel behind a bathtub or shower. Removing the panel reveals the plumbing. Note from which directions the supply pipes enter the wall. Record the locations of any valves you come across.

Some older homes have hot water heat supplied from a boiler. Map these lines separately.

MAPPING SYMBOLS

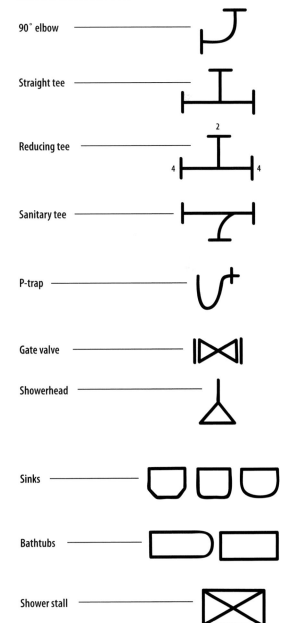

90° elbow

Straight tee

Reducing tee

Sanitary tee

P-trap

Gate valve

Showerhead

Sinks

Bathtubs

Shower stall

Mapping your system *(continued)*

Locate the water meter

Know the location of the water meter. You'll find the main shutoff valve for the house adjacent to it. Some homes have shutoff valves on both sides of the meter. If you don't see a shutoff valve near the water meter, follow the line to where it enters your house. There should be a shutoff valve located along it. In warm climates, the shutoff valve might be located on the outside of the home, sometimes in a plastic or concrete box called a buffalo box. Homes built in colder regions may have the main shutoff valve buried below the frost line. A key is used to reach the valve through a valve box above the valve. If you still can't locate the shutoff, contact your local municipal water supplier. Once you locate the meter and shutoff valve, measure and mark both locations using the proper plumbing symbols.

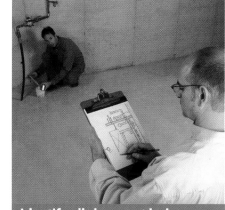

Identify all clean-out hubs

Older homes have main stacks of cast-iron construction; newer home construction uses plastic pipe for the stacks and drain/waste system. Stacks usually run straight through the roof. You'll find a cleanout hub near the lowest point of the stack. You may also find cleanouts along the drainpipe runs. Include all cleanouts on your map. Note the location of each with measurements. Should the pipes have a backup or blockage, these locations will make clearing out the blockage easier.

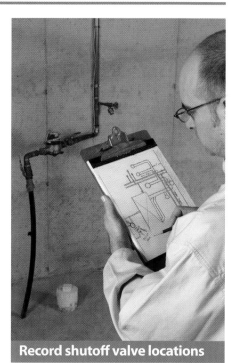

Record shutoff valve locations

Seek out the locations of all shutoff valves in your home. Record them on your map. In an emergency such as a burst pipe, you will be able to quickly find the valve and shut off the water.

FINDING HIDDEN PIPES

Follow these steps to find pipes that run behind walls or through enclosed floors and ceilings:

- Determine which valves control which fixtures by closing the valves. Check which fixtures do not have water.
- Most basic interior walls are approximately 4 inches thick. If you find a wall that is thicker, it probably contains a main vent stack.
- Locating secondary stacks can be difficult. Have a helper feed an auger down the roof vent while you locate the sound from inside.
- Use the distinctive sounds pipes make to assist in identifying them. Drainpipes make a gurgling sound and supply pipes make more of a hissing sound. An old plumber's trick to locate and determine which is which is to place the open end of a drinking glass against the wall. Put your ear on the bottom of the glass. The glass magnifies sound.

Measure and record all pipe runs

Mark the location of supply and wastewater pipes as they run horizontally along floor joists and vertically (called a riser) into the floor above. As you follow a horizontally run pipe, remember that it's not unusual for pipe to change from horizontal to vertical and back again.

TROUBLESHOOTING AND REPAIRS

Troubleshooting main valve lines

- **TIME:** About 1 hour
- **SKILLS:** No special skills needed
- **TOOLS:** Screwdriver, adjustable wrench, groove-joint pliers, pipe wrench

In older homes, the shutoff valves for the main line often are worn and rusted. If you have a shutoff up-line (closer to the water main) from the valve, you can easily shut off the water and replace the valve. If not, your options are to live with a less-than-perfect valve or pay the water company to shut off your water while you change valves.

If the shutoff valve handle breaks off in such a way that you cannot easily replace it, use pliers or a pipe wrench to turn the valve off and on. If you want to make sure all household members can turn off the water in case of an emergency, however, you'll eventually have to replace the valve.

These valves also commonly leak from the packing nut whether the valve is open or closed. To fix it, tighten the nut gently. Don't apply too much force when tightening or the valve may crack. If a slow drip continues, place a bucket under it and watch it for a day or two—sometimes the leak stops on its own.

If not, you will need to repack the valve. Make sure the valve is shut off. Turn it clockwise until it tightens. Unscrew the screw at the top and remove the handle. Loosen and remove the packing nut. Apply strand packing or a packing washer (see page 17) and reinstall the packing nut.

You can purchase valves that screw onto galvanized pipe or brass adapters, or solder onto copper lines.

Gate valve

This style of valve, commonly found in older houses, is not as reliable as a globe or ball valve, so replace it if you have the opportunity. A wedge-shaped brass "gate" screws up and down to control water flow. If it does not fully stop water flow, it cannot be repaired. To repair a leak around the handle, replace the packing washer or strand packing.

Globe valve

This works in much the same way stem faucets do (see page 15). It is more reliable and more easily repaired than a gate valve. If it does not fully stop water and you can shut off the flow prior to the valve, replace the stem washer. To repair a leak around the handle, replace the packing washer.

Ball valve

This costs more than the other valves but is more reliable and is easy to shut off quickly. The lever rotates a ball-like gate pierced by an opening. The gate pivots to control the flow of water.

AVOID CLOGGING FAUCETS

Rust, lime, and sediment deposits build up inside pipes over time. When you shut off water and turn it back on in a house that has old galvanized pipe, these deposits loosen and flow through the pipes. After turning off the main valve, take time to remove aerators from the faucets and let the water run for a couple of minutes to flush out the gunk.

Identifying stem faucets

When a faucet develops a leak—most often, a drip from the spout or a leak around the base—the problem is usually easy to fix. It's highly likely that you can purchase a repair kit for your type of faucet. Repair techniques vary from faucet to faucet, but in most cases you can easily do it yourself. When buying replacement parts, take the old unit to the store. If the faucet cannot be repaired, it's easy to replace it with a new one (see pages 92–94).

The first step is to identify the type of faucet you have. The anatomy drawings here and on pages 20, 22, 24, and 26 show the various types.

The seat-and-washer faucet, often called a compression faucet, is the most common. Stem faucets have separate hot and cold controls. In the "off" (closed) position, the stem compresses a resilient washer on the stem into a beveled seat located in the faucet base, stopping the flow of water.

As the washer wears, you have to apply more and more pressure to turn off the unit. That's when dripping usually begins.

Two newer faucet styles, cartridge and diaphragm, eliminate washers altogether. The cartridge type rotates to control flow. It uses a rubber seal and O-rings. The diaphragm faucet uses a durable diaphragm in lieu of a resilient washer.

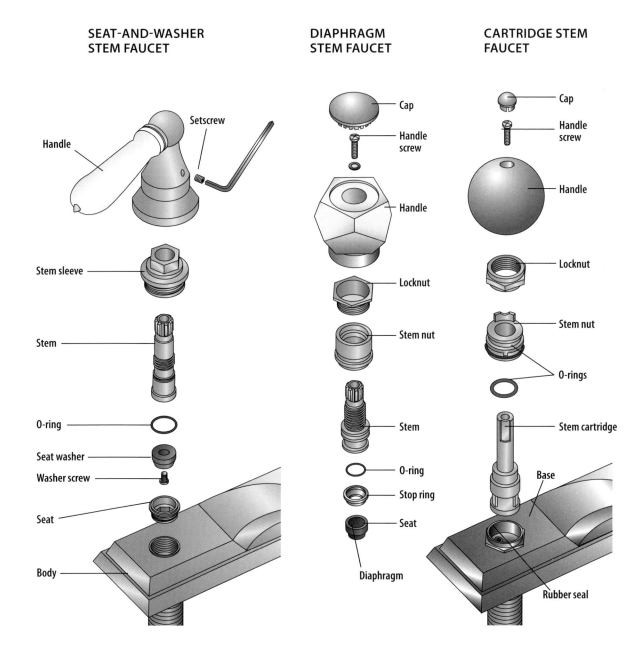

SEAT-AND-WASHER STEM FAUCET

Handle · Setscrew · Stem sleeve · Stem · O-ring · Seat washer · Washer screw · Seat · Body

DIAPHRAGM STEM FAUCET

Cap · Handle screw · Handle · Locknut · Stem nut · Stem · O-ring · Stop ring · Seat · Diaphragm

CARTRIDGE STEM FAUCET

Cap · Handle screw · Handle · Locknut · Stem nut · O-rings · Stem cartridge · Base · Rubber seal

Pulling out handles and stems

- **TIME:** About 15 minutes, unless the parts are stuck
- **SKILLS:** No special skills needed
- **TOOLS:** Screwdriver, tongue-and-groove pliers, possibly a handle puller

The first step in replacing the inner workings of a stem faucet is to shut off the water supply at the nearest stop valve. Pull out the handles and stems. Take them to the store so you're sure to buy proper replacement parts. If you can identify the faucet's brand name, parts will be easier to find. Often no brand name is visible, so you'll have to take out the stem and compare it with the drawings on pages 15, 20, 22, 24, and 26.

1 Remove cap and screw

If the handle is round, it is probably connected to the stem with a screw from the top. You may have to pry off a cap (usually marked "H" or "C") to get to it. Some handles are attached with setscrews—see the handle on the seat-and-washer stem faucet on page 15. Remove the setscrew with an allen wrench and pull off the handle.

2 Pull out handle and stem

Usually the handle will come out if you pull it up firmly or pry it up with a screwdriver. Take care not to mar the finish. If it is stuck, use a handle puller, a tool that grips the handle from underneath and draws the handle off the stem. Once the handle is off, unscrew the stem with a wrench or pliers.

Replacing seat washers

- **TIME:** About 30 minutes, plus a trip to a plumbing supplier if you don't have a replacement washer
- **SKILLS:** No special skills needed
- **TOOLS:** Screwdriver

The washers in seat-and-washer stem faucets often become worn. Most commonly, there is a depression running in a ring around the washer, or the washer has begun to crumble with old age.

If a washer you replaced wears out quickly, the seat is probably damaged and nicks the washer when you shut the water off. This causes the faucet to drip. (See page 19 to replace a seat.)

1 Remove the old washer

Examine your washer. If it is damaged in any way, remove the washer screw and pull off the old washer. Clean away any debris or deposits from the bottom of the stem. Take the stem and old washer to the store with you.

2 Insert a new washer

Find a washer the exact same size and shape as the old one. If the old washer is deformed, this may be difficult to determine, so slip the new washer onto the bottom of the stem to double-check. The right fit is snug. Replace and tighten the screw and reinstall the stem.

Repairing diaphragm and cartridge stems

- **TIME:** About 1 hour to remove the faucet handle, unscrew the stem, and replace parts
- **SKILLS:** No special skills needed
- **TOOLS:** Small screwdriver or a sharp-pointed tool

Diaphragm and cartridge stem faucets are as easy to repair as seat-and-washer stem faucets. Often the most difficult part of the job is to find the right parts. There are hundreds of O-ring sizes. To avoid mistakes, remove the stem, take it to your supplier, and show it to a salesperson.

Be sure to shut off the water supply before removing stems.

Replace a diaphragm

Sometimes called a top hat stem, a diaphragm stem has a diaphragm that functions much like a seat washer. To replace it, pull off the worn diaphragm and snap on a new one.

Replace the O-ring, seal, and spring

To fix a leaky cartridge stem, replace the seal and O-rings. Remove the rubber seal from the base of the faucet with the end of a pencil; a small spring will come out as well. Remove the O-ring by hand or carefully pry it off with a sharp tool. Lubricate the new parts lightly with heatproof grease after you install them.

Repairing leaks around handles

- **TIME:** About 15 minutes to repack a spindle and replace an O-ring
- **SKILLS:** No special skills needed
- **TOOLS:** None

If the faucet leaks around the handle, you'll need to remove the stem to get at the source of the problem. The spindles of older faucets have packing wound around the top to keep water from seeping out. Don't be put off by this old-fashioned material; it is easy to replace, and new packing lasts for years. Newer stems have O-rings. Once you get the stem out, inspect the rest of the faucet and replace any parts that look as if they're starting to wear.

Shut off the water supply.

Wrap new packing string

If your faucet has packing wound around the spindle just under the packing nut (see page 14), remove all of it and clean the spindle. Choose either plumber's tape or strand packing and wind it fairly tight. Leave just enough room to screw on the packing nut when the stem is replaced.

Replace the O-ring

Newer stems utilize an O-ring instead of packing. Simply remove the old O-ring and replace it with one that fits exactly. Lightly lubricate the O-ring with heatproof grease after you install it and before you reinstall the stem.

Replacing and grinding seats

■ **TIME:** About 20 minutes to replace or grind a seat, once you have the part or tool

■ **SKILLS:** No special skills needed, but you must work carefully

■ **TOOLS:** Flashlight, seat wrench or seat cutter

If you have a leaky faucet, inspect the entire faucet to be certain you repair everything responsible for the leak. Otherwise you may implement what you think is a quick fix, only to find that the faucet still leaks.

When the spout of a stem faucet (either a seat-and-washer or a diaphragm type) leaks, inspect the seat as well as the washer or diaphragm. If the seat is pitted or scored, it is scraping the washer or diaphragm every time you turn off the faucet. It will quickly damage a new seat washer, and your faucet will leak again even if you think you fixed the problem.

If the seat is damaged, it is best to replace it, though sometimes it is hard to extract. In this case, try grinding it smooth with a special tool called a seat grinder made for resurfacing faucet seats. A smooth seat won't damage other parts, and the faucet will no longer leak.

If you need to replace one valve seat in a two-handle faucet, go ahead and replace the other handle's valve seat as well. It's sure to start leaking soon, and replacing both now will save you time in the long run.

Remove the handle

Shut off the water supply. Lower the sink stopper and cover it with a cloth to avoid losing loose parts down the drain. Pry off the handle cap. Remove the handle using a screwdriver.

Seat washer

Inspect the seat

Remove the stem and inspect the washer or diaphragm. If it looks cut up, the likely cause is a damaged seat. Whether or not the washer or diaphragm looks damaged, examine the seat: First look at it with a flashlight, then feel it with your finger. If it appears or feels less than smooth, the washer or diaphragm will fail to seal off water when you crank down on the handle. Replace the seat or grind it smooth with a seat cutter.

Seat wrench

Replace a damaged seat

Though it is sometimes possible to remove a seat with a screwdriver, attempting to do so is risky. You may damage the seat so badly it cannot be removed. Instead purchase a seat wrench, which is designed to remove seats of various sizes. Insert it into the seat, push down firmly, and turn counterclockwise. Install the new seat with the same tool.

Stem nut

Cutter head

1 Use a seat grinder for a seat that cannot be removed

Purchase a seat grinder. Slip the stem nut over the shaft of the seat cutter—it helps stabilize the grinder. Select a cutter head that fits easily inside the body and is as wide as the seat.

Stem nut

2 Rotate the washer

Screw the stem nut into the faucet body to hold the shaft securely without wobbling. Push down gently and turn the handle clockwise three full rotations. Remove the grinder and inspect the seat with a flashlight. If it is not smooth, try again. When you're done, flush any debris that resulted from grinding: Either hold a rag over the opening and gently open the supply valve, or blow out the debris with compressed air. Reassemble the faucet.

Repairing cartridge faucets

■ **TIME:** About 1 hour, once you have the replacement parts
■ **SKILLS:** No special skills needed
■ **TOOLS:** Screwdriver, needle-nose and groove-joint pliers

Most of the faucets that work without washers use a combination of seals and O-rings to control and direct water. A cartridge faucet is one example.

In the type shown, the cartridge O-rings fit snugly against the inside of the faucet body. One O-ring forms a seal between the hot and cold supply lines. The others protect against leaks from the spout and from under the handle. On swivel-spout models, another ring protects against leaks from under the spout. Raising the handle lifts the stem so it slides upward inside the cartridge. Holes in the stem align with the openings in the cartridge in various combinations.

Other types of cartridge faucets have fewer O-rings and use other types of seals. Repair kits are available for each manufacturer and model.

When a cartridge faucet leaks, you can replace either the O-rings or the cartridge itself, if it has corroded. Because the design is simple, repairs don't take long. In fact, disassembly usually makes for the bulk of the work. Be sure to find an exact match for the retainer clip that holds the cartridge in the faucet.

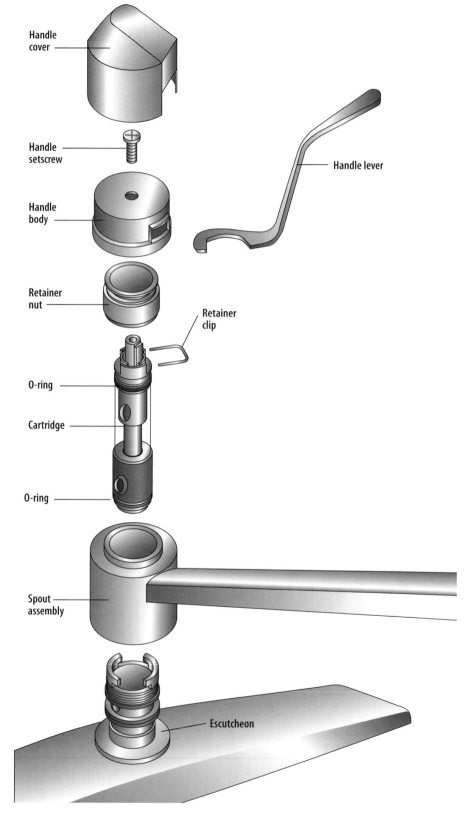

Handle cover

Handle setscrew

Handle body

Handle lever

Retainer nut

Retainer clip

O-ring

Cartridge

O-ring

Spout assembly

Escutcheon

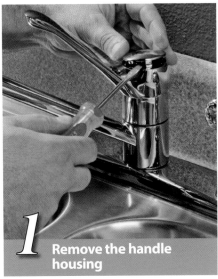

1 Remove the handle housing

Shut off the water and drain the line.
Cartridge faucets vary in design from model to model, but you disassemble most of them as follows: Pry off the cover that conceals the handle screw. Be careful not to crack the cover in doing so—most are made of plastic. You may need to remove an external retaining clip to get the cover off.

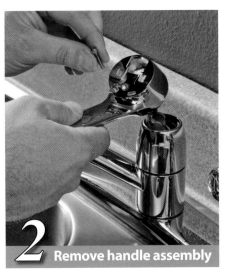

2 Remove handle assembly

Cover the drain with a rag to avoid losing small parts. A setscrew that holds the handle in place is located beneath the handle housing. Remove the handle screw and lift off the handle body and lever. If there is no retainer nut, lift out the spout. Otherwise, proceed to Step 3.

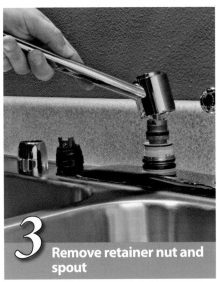

3 Remove retainer nut and spout

Swivel-spout models have a retainer nut. Unscrew it, then lift it off the spout.

Some models come apart differently. Pry off the cap on top of the faucet, remove the screw, and tilt back and pull up the handle to remove it. Then remove the plastic threaded retaining ring.

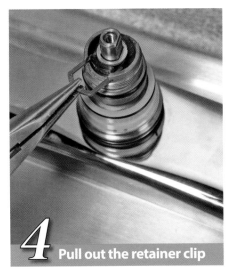

4 Pull out the retainer clip

Depending on the model, you may need to lift off a cylindrical sleeve to get at the cartridge. Without the sleeve, you should be able to see the retainer clip, a metal piece that holds the cartridge in place. Use needle-nose pliers to remove the clip from its slot. Be careful not to misplace it.

5 Remove the cartridge

With pliers, lift the cartridge from the faucet body. Take note of the position of the cartridge ears (when you put the cartridge back in, its ears must face the same direction or hot and cold will be reversed). Before you replace the O-rings, give them a light coating of heatproof grease. When reassembling the faucet, tighten firmly but don't crank down hard—its plastic parts can crack easily.

BUY QUALITY REPLACEMENT PARTS

Your local hardware store or building supply center may have replacement parts that are inexpensive but a bit flimsy. As long as you are investing a fair amount of your time in making the repair, it's to your benefit to pay the relatively small extra cost to install long-lasting parts. It is usually best to buy replacement parts made by the faucet manufacturer, rather than by a general supplier that makes only replacement parts.

If you can't find the manufacturer's name on the faucet, remove the parts and take them to your supplier to ensure the right match.

Repairing rotating ball faucets

■ **TIME:** About 2 hours to rebuild and reassemble a faucet

■ **SKILLS:** No special skills needed

■ **TOOLS:** Adjustable pliers, allen wrench, wrench that comes with the rebuild kit, awl or another pointed tool

Inside a rotating ball faucet, a slotted ball sits on top of a pair of spring-loaded seals. When the handle is lowered to the "off" position, this ball, held tight against the seals by the faucet's cap, closes off the water supply.

As the handle is raised, the ball rotates in such a way that the openings align with the supply line ports. This allows water to pass through the ball and out the spout. Moving the handle to the left allows more hot water to flow out; moving it to the right draws cold water.

Most leaks are the result of a faulty ball and/or gaskets. Seals and springs also give out and need replacement.

A leak around the handle or under the base of the spout (in swivel-spout models) indicates that the adjusting ring has loosened or the seal above the ball is worn.

Leaks under the spout result from O-ring failure. Inspect the rings that encircle the body. Also, on units that have diverter valves for a sprayer, inspect the valve O-ring. Replace it if it looks worn.

CAUTION

TURN OFF SUPPLY LINES

To avoid damage to flooring and walls, turn off the stop valves in the supply lines or the main water valve.

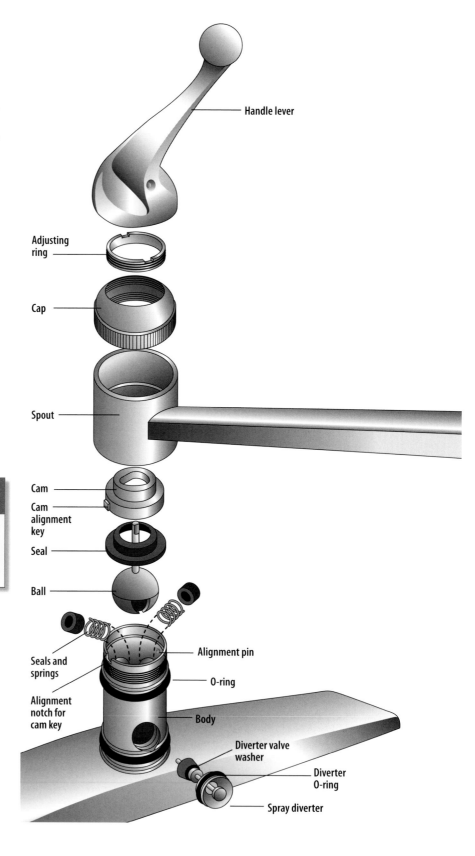

Handle lever

Adjusting ring

Cap

Spout

Cam

Cam alignment key

Seal

Ball

Seals and springs

Alignment notch for cam key

Alignment pin

O-ring

Body

Diverter valve washer

Diverter O-ring

Spray diverter

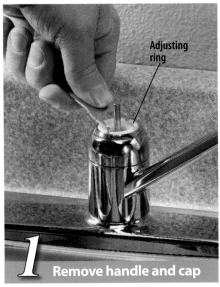

1   Remove handle and cap

Shut off the water supply and lift straight up on the handle to drain the lines. Using an allen wrench, loosen the setscrew that holds the handle in place. Loosen the adjusting ring with the wrench that came with your purchased repair kit.

2   Disassemble cam, ball, and spout

Unscrew the cap with cloth- or tape-covered adjustable pliers. Lift out the cam assembly, the ball, and the spout (in the case of a swivel-spout faucet). The spout fits tightly against the O-rings of the body, so it may prove stubborn. Be careful not to scratch the spout as you remove it.

3   Remove seals and springs

To remove worn seals and springs from the body, use a pencil to fish them out. Check for blockage at the supply inlet ports, scrape away any buildup, then insert new springs and seals.

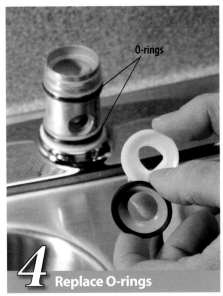

4   Replace O-rings

If the faucet has a swivel spout, pry the O-rings away from the body using an awl or other pointed tool. Roll the new ones down over the body until they rest in the appropriate grooves. Replace the diverter O-ring in the same way. Lightly coat the O-rings and the inside of the spout with heatproof grease.

5   Reassemble

Be sure to align the slot in the side of the ball with the pin inside the body. The key on the cam assembly also fits into a corresponding notch in the body. Hand-tighten the cap and tighten the adjusting ring to create a good seal between the ball and the cam. If it leaks, tighten further.

SELECT QUALITY PARTS

You'll find repair kits of lesser and greater quality for this type of faucet. Some come with plastic balls; others have longer-lasting metal parts. If your hardware store offers the cheaper kit only, go to a plumbing supply store and ask for a kit that has longer-lasting (though more expensive) parts.

CONSIDER A COMPLETE REBUILD
When one faucet part is old enough to wear out, other parts will soon follow. If you're going to fix one part of the faucet, you might consider rebuilding it completely.

Repairing ceramic disk faucets

■ **TIME:** About 1 hour for repairs
■ **SKILLS:** No special skills needed
■ **TOOLS:** Small screwdriver, groove-joint pliers, large screwdriver, pointed tool

When you raise the faucet lever of a disk faucet, the upper disk in the cartridge slides across the lower disk, allowing water to enter the mixing chamber. The higher you raise the lever, the more water enters through the inlet ports of the faucet body. Moving the lever from side to side determines whether hot or cold water, or a mixture of the two, comes out of the spout.

The disk assembly, generally made of a long-lasting ceramic material, rarely needs replacing. Over time, however, mineral deposits can clog the inlet ports. If this happens, disassemble the faucet and scrape away the crusty buildup.

If the faucet leaks at the base of the lever, one or more of the inlet seals on the cartridge may need replacing. While the faucet is dismantled, it's a smart idea to replace all the seals. If one is worn, the others don't have long to live. Before making the trip to the hardware store, get the brand name of your faucet from the faucet body (or take the disk assembly along). A repair kit with the parts you need is likely available.

Lever

Cartridge screw

Post

Cartridge

Inlet seal

Body

Spout

1 Remove the lever and cap

Cap

Cartridge

Shut off the water supply. Under the lever, a setscrew holds the lever to the lever post. Use a screwdriver to unscrew the setscrew—don't try to unscrew it with a knife because you may damage it. Loosen the screw until you can raise the lever off the post. You may have to gently pry it off with a large screwdriver.

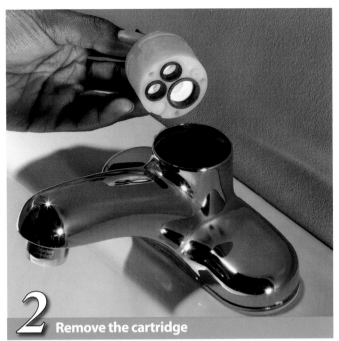

2 Remove the cartridge

Lift off or unscrew the decorative cap that covers the cartridge. Loosen the screws holding the cartridge to the faucet body and lift out the cartridge.

3 Remove the seals

Seals

You'll find a set of seals on the underside of the cartridge. Pull them out with your fingers, or carefully use a pointed tool, being careful not to scratch the cartridge.

4 Clean the openings

Check the openings for sediment buildup. If you find any, use a nonmetallic scrubber or a sponge to clean the openings.

5 Replace the seals and reassemble

Cartridge

Seal

Put the old seals back or install replacement seals. Reassemble the faucet. Turn the water back on and test. If the faucet continues to leak after you have cleaned the cartridge and replaced the seals, install a new cartridge.

Repairing gasket cartridge faucets

■ **TIME:** About 1 hour, plus shopping time
■ **SKILLS:** Basic plumbing skills
■ **TOOLS:** Screwdriver, groove-joint pliers

Gasket cartridge faucets use a gasket with a group of openings at the bottom of the faucet cartridge to mix hot and cold water and direct water to the spout. Newer faucet models have ceramic cartridges; older ones have plastic.

Shut off the water supply before disassembling.

If you're trying to fix a leak from the body of the faucet, first tighten the cap by hand—do not use a wrench. If that doesn't work, disassemble the faucet and replace the two O-rings. Coat them lightly with heatproof grease.

To disassemble, pry off the cap and remove the lever screw. Lift off the lever and unscrew the housing and the retainer nut. The other parts pull out.

If the spout drips, the cartridge probably needs to be replaced. Check the threads on the retainer nut as well. If they're stripped, replace the nut.

These parts are specific to the faucet manufacturer, so take the old parts with you to the store to make sure you buy the right replacements.

If the faucet operates stiffly, debris may have built up in the cartridge. In most cases, replace the cartridge. It's more trouble to clean than it is to buy a new one.

Cap

Lever screw

Lever

Housing

Spout

O-rings

Aerator

Retainer nut

Cartridge

Gasket (attached to cartridge)

Faucet body

Split ring

Baseplate

Sealing leaky baseplates

- **TIME:** 2 hours to remove, seal, and replace the faucet
- **SKILLS:** Basic plumbing skills
- **TOOLS:** Putty knife, groove-joint pliers or basin wrench

If you find water in the cabinet below the sink, it could have come from three places: the supply lines, the drain, or a leak under the faucet baseplate. Tightening the supply lines may solve the problem (see page 29). If the leak comes from the drain, see page 49. If neither is the cause, the sink may have a leaky baseplate that allows splashed water to seep through mounting holes. If so, follow the steps on this page.

1 Tighten the mounting nuts

It may be that your faucet is not held tightly against the sink. Get under your sink in as comfortable a position as possible and tighten the mounting nuts. If you can't turn them with pliers, use a basin wrench (see page 92). If this doesn't solve the problem, try Step 2.

2 Loosen, stuff with putty

First try to fix the leak without removing the faucet. Loosen the mounting nuts enough to raise the faucet base about ½ inch above the sink. Scrape out any hardened old putty. Holding the baseplate just above the sink, stuff plumber's putty under it evenly. Retighten the mounting nuts. If it continues to leak, proceed to Step 3.

3 Remove the faucet and scrape

Shut off the water and drain the line. To entirely reseat the baseplate, remove the faucet. Disconnect the supply lines, remove the mounting nuts, and pull out the faucet. Scrape any old putty away and clean the area thoroughly. Take care not to scratch the sink.

4 Replace the gasket ...

If the faucet has a gasket, throw it out and replace it with a new one. If you have trouble finding a replacement, purchase a piece of rubber of a similar thickness and make your own gasket. Use the old gasket as a pattern to cut out a new one.

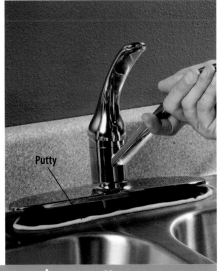

or apply new putty

Many plumbers believe putty lasts longer than gaskets, so even if your faucet has a gasket, you may want to discard it and apply putty instead. Roll a rope of putty about ¼ inch in diameter and apply it to the sink or to the underside of the faucet. Reinstall the faucet and check for leaks.

Fixing sprayers, diverters, and aerators

- **TIME:** 1 to 2 hours
- **SKILLS:** Basic plumbing skills and attention to detail
- **TOOLS:** Groove-joint pliers, old toothbrush, awl, or toothpick

Sink sprayers can become obstructed at the connections, gaskets, and nozzle. If water fails to come out of the sprayer, the problem is most likely a faulty diverter valve. You can replace either the rubber seal or the diverter. Remove the diverter and take it to your supplier to make sure you get the correct replacement.

Diverters vary in shape and location, but all work in much the same way. When water flows toward the spray outlet, the valve remains open and directs the water flow toward the spout. When you press the sprayer lever, the flow of water shifts toward the sprayer head.

If the water pressure in your faucet is low, check the aerator. Aerators develop leaks when their seals are worn, and they can become clogged.

TROUBLESHOOT THE SPRAYER

Minerals may be restricting the flow of water through the sprayer. Clean the spray disk with an awl or a toothpick as shown below. Replace worn parts and tighten all connections.

From diverter to sprayer

To find the diverter in a typical one-handle faucet, remove the spout; it's usually located in front. If the sprayer has low or no water pressure, check the hose for kinks. A slow stream of water coupled with some water coming from the spout signals a stuck valve or a worn washer or O-ring. Replace the rubber parts or the diverter valve. Check the sprayer screen as well; it may be clogged (see below).

Clean the aerator

To clean out the aerator, unscrew it from the faucet spout. Disassemble it, brush all the parts clean, and soak the pieces in vinegar overnight. If it is heavily clogged, you'll need to buy a new one.

Stopping leaks in flexible supply lines

- **TIME:** 1 hour for most repairs and replacements
- **SKILLS:** Tightening and loosening nuts in tight places
- **TOOLS:** Basin wrench or groove-joint pliers, adjustable wrenches

Two basic types of flexible supply lines are available—tubing or braided hoses. Plain and corrugated copper tubing and plastic tubing require ferrules and nuts for connections to the stop valve. The fixture end differs for faucets or toilets. Braided flexible supply lines—either plastic or stainless steel— have attached nuts (different for faucets or toilets) at one end and nuts for stop valves at the other. Braided lines are the easiest to use. Make sure you buy lines of an appropriate length.

VERIFY WHERE IT'S LEAKING FIRST

Water dripping off the stop valve and a wet nut where the supply line connects to the valve might look at first like a loose valve connection. But before you start work, feel along the length of the supply tube; if it is wet, the leak is probably at the top where the supply tube connects to the faucet. Tighten those connections as shown on page 94.

1 Tighten the nuts

Often the solution is as simple as tightening the nut at the point where you see a leak. Take care not to overtighten— you can crack the nut or strip the threads. Use only adjustable wrenches, not pipe wrenches. If the leak persists, loosen the nuts and recoat the threads or ferrules with plumber's tape or pipe joint compound as shown in Step 2.

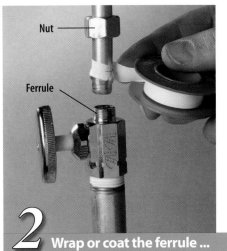

Nut

Ferrule

2 Wrap or coat the ferrule ...

Shut off the water and drain the line. If you are working with a tubing-and-ferrule connection, remove the nut and pull the line out of the valve. Take care not to kink it. Wrap the ferrule with plumber's joint tape or coat it with joint compound. Hook it back up, tighten, and test.

or the threads

If you are working with a plastic or braided flexible line, shut off the water, unscrew the nut, and apply joint compound or joint tape to the male threads of the shutoff valve or the faucet. Reconnect, tighten, and test.

3 Install a new line

If these measures fail to solve your problem quickly, it could be the fault of the old line. Shut off the water and remove the old supply line. Buy a new flexible line, apply joint tape or joint compound to the male threads, and screw it on. Tighten both ends and test.

Repairing tub and shower controls

- **TIME:** About 2 hours for most repairs, plus time spent looking for parts
- **SKILLS:** Basic plumbing skills and ability to work with tile
- **TOOLS:** Screwdriver, pliers, wrenches

Tub and shower controls work much the same way sink faucets do, so their repairs involve many of the same operations (except that you have to work horizontally rather than vertically). However, tub and shower controls are more complicated because, in addition to mixing hot and cold water, they divert water both to the tub spout and to the showerhead. The anatomy drawings on these pages show the inner workings of common types.

Sometimes tub and shower parts are hard to reach. You may have to chip away at tiles in order to get your tools where they need to go.

If a shower control body is damaged and needs to be replaced, check the opposite side of the wall to see if there's an access panel. If so, you may be able to work from there, minimizing damage to your shower wall. Otherwise the job of replacing a shower control body means tearing up a shower wall and retiling.

Be sure to shut off the supply stop valves, built-in shutoff valves, or the main water valve before making repairs.

Choosing fixtures

Choose from a vast selection of styles and features when replacing a tub or shower faucet. Finding a match for your tastes and needs is easy. Many options exist thanks to new technologies in metallurgy, which have created durable finishes.

One-handle ball control

This type of control has seals and springs like rotating ball sink faucets, so repairs are similar to those shown on pages 22–23. As the handle is raised, the ball rotates in such a way that its openings align with the supply line ports, allowing water to pass through the ball and out the spout.

Impeded flow is usually the result of clogged orifices or worn seals. Shut off the water and remove the ball—some ball controls have setscrews that you have to remove to do this. Clean out the orifices, replace worn rubber parts and lubricate them with heatproof grease.

While you have the faucet apart, check the ball for wear and corrosion. If it's worn, replace it with a new one.

ONE-HANDLE BALL CONTROL

Shower control body · Orifice · Ball · Seal · Cam · Cap · O-ring · Seal and spring · Escutcheon · Handle

ONE-HANDLE CARTRIDGE CONTROL

Cartridge

Shower
control
body

Retaining
clip

Retainer
nut

Handle

One-handle cartridge control

One-handle cartridge controls take many forms besides the one shown here, so use the diagram above as a general guide. You may have to search out the location of your parts, such as the retaining clip. Parts are usually made of plastic; be careful not to crack them.

To repair a leak or impeded flow, remove the handle, unscrew the retainer nut, and pull out the cartridge. Clean away deposits and replace worn rubber or plastic parts. Lubricate all rubber parts with heatproof grease.

Or replace the cartridge itself. When you remove the old cartridge, be sure to note its original position, and insert the new one the same way. Otherwise hot and cold water will be reversed.

See pages 20–21 for more on repairing cartridge faucets.

Dual control
This dual shower employs both a one-handle cartridge control for the rain-type showerhead, and a two-handle control for the hand shower.

Repairing tub and shower controls *(continued)*

TWO-HANDLE CONTROL

Shower control body

Seat washer

O-ring

Stem

Packing nut

Handle

Handle cap

Diverter valve

Spout

Two-handle control

Two-handle controls usually contain stems with washers. Like their sink faucet counterparts, each washer presses against a seat in order to shut the water off (see pages 15–19). To stop a drip, shut off the water, and remove the stem—you may have to use a special stem wrench or a deep socket wrench, or chip away at the tiles to get to the packing nut. Replace the washer and the seat, if necessary, the same way you would on a sink faucet (see page 16). If the diverter valve on the spout is not working properly, replace the spout.

Achieve retro style
This two-handle control complements the retro styling of this bath. Here, the diverter valve directs water to a hand shower (not shown) to rinse off after a soak in the whirlpool.

THREE-HANDLE CONTROL

Shower control body

To showerhead

Escutcheon

Diverter

Handle cap

Seat

Seat washer

Stem

Packing washer

Packing nut

Escutcheon

Handle

Handle cap

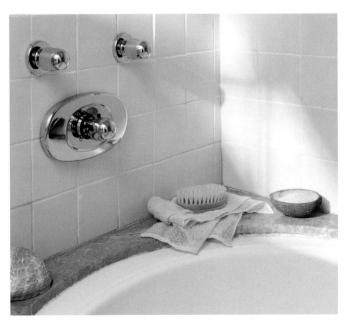

Three-handle control

The three-handle control works like a two-handle control, but it has a central handle that controls a diverter valve. The valve directs water either up or down—out the showerhead or out the spout. If the diverter valve sticks or does not completely divert water to the showerhead or spout, shut off the water, and remove the stem just as you would a regular stem (see page 16). Take it apart, clean it, and replace any washers or O-rings (see pages 16–17). Or replace the whole stem with a new one.

Take control

Three-handle fixtures provide a simple way to control water temperature and water flow for a tub and shower combination.

Cleaning showerheads

■ **TIME:** About 1 hour for removal and scrubbing; overnight soaking for a thorough cleaning
■ **SKILLS:** Basic plumbing skills
■ **TOOLS:** Wrench, screwdriver, pointed tool or thin wire, toothbrush

If your showerhead sprays unevenly, you can either clean it or replace it. If it leaks at the arm, or if it doesn't stay in position, tighten the retainer or collar nut. If that doesn't work, replace the O-ring—or replace the showerhead.

If you want to replace your showerhead, take the old one with you to your supplier to make sure you get one that will fit the arm or pipe. You'll find a wide range of styles and features.

CLEAN THE HOLES

Showerheads spray unevenly when the tiny holes have gotten clogged with mineral deposits. Use an old toothbrush to clean the head. Then run a sharp blast of water backward through the showerhead.

DISMANTLE AND CLEAN

For a thorough cleaning, take the head apart, use a pin to poke out any mineral buildup or debris, and brush away all deposits. Then soak the parts in vinegar overnight to dissolve remaining mineral deposits. Reassemble and reinstall.

Flange

Shower arm

Showerhead

Swivel ball

Collar

Rubber gasket

Spray outlets

Spray adjuster

Shower arm

Nut

Removing a showerhead

This is a simple matter of unscrewing the nut at the shower arm. Take care not to mar the finish of the showerhead or arm: Use a wrench rather than pliers, and as an added precaution, cushion your tool with a rag or tape as you work.

Two basic types

Newer showerheads screw onto the shower arm, the chrome pipe that extends from the wall. Older models require a shower arm with a ball-shape end that acts as a swivel. In most cases, you can switch to a newer style if you replace the shower arm. To do so, remove the shower arm from its connection. Wrap plumber's tape around the threads of the new shower arm before screwing it into place.

Maintaining a clothes washer

- **TIME:** Approximately 1 hour, plus time to soak overnight
- **SKILLS:** Basic plumbing skills
- **TOOLS:** Groove-joint pliers, toothbrush, needle-nose pliers or tweezers

Clothes washers are designed to be durable and last 10 to 15 years. Keeping them in good working condition requires periodic maintenance. Most washer surfaces are coated with a porcelain enamel, which is very resistant to staining. However, long-term exposure to chemicals can damage the appliance's surfaces. Promptly wipe up any spills with a damp cloth or paper towel.

As a rule, replace inlet hoses every five years. Periodically inspect and replace the hoses if bulges, kinks, cuts, wear, or leaks are discovered.

If you won't be using your washer for an extended period of time, give it a break. Unplug the washer and turn off the water supply. This reduces the likelihood that a hose will burst and flood your house while you are away. Leave the lid or door slightly ajar to provide ventilation.

Depending on the hardness of your water supply, plan on cleaning or replacing the washer's inlet screens. Sediment builds up over time, clogging the flow of water to the machine.

1 Disconnect the hoses

Unplug the washer and move it away from the wall so you can access the hose connections at the back of the washer. Turn off the valves that control hot and cold water flowing to the hoses. Use pliers to unscrew and disconnect the hoses. Drain water in the hoses into a bucket or the floor drain.

2 Remove the screens

Use tweezers or needle-nose pliers to pry out the inlet screens. Inlet screens prevent debris from entering the washer. If you rip or crinkle a screen, or if you don't want to bother with cleaning, replace both screens. They are available at hardware stores and home centers.

3 Clean and replace the screens

If the screens are crusted with mineral deposits, soak them overnight in vinegar or a cleaning product made for loosening hard water buildup. Use an old toothbrush to clean any remaining deposits. Rinse with running water until the screen is completely clean.

Use tweezers or needle-nose pliers to carefully reposition the inlet screens in the washer.

Attach the hot and cold water lines to the inlet openings. Screw the hoses back on, then tighten with groove-joint pliers. Turn the water on and check for leaks; you may need to tighten the hose connections further. Push the washer back in place and check to make sure it is level. Add shims or adjust the feet under the washer until it's level.

Fixing toilet tank run-on

- **TIME:** 5 minutes to adjust the float; 30 minutes to adjust and clean the flush valve; 1 hour to replace a ballcock
- **SKILLS:** No special skills needed
- **TOOLS:** Screwdriver, groove-joint pliers

Most of a toilet's mechanical action goes on inside the flush tank, which is why most common toilet problems develop there. If water continually trickles or flows into the tank and/or bowl, start with the simplest diagnosis: The float may be rising too high. This causes water to trickle down the overflow tube. If fixing that doesn't solve the problem, see if the chain is tangled or has fallen off. Then check the flapper and ballcock.

CHECK THE FLOAT FOR DAMAGE

A cracked float ball takes on water and can't rise enough to trip the ballcock. To test it, agitate the ball. A faulty ball makes a swishing sound. Unscrew a faulty float ball and replace it with a new one.

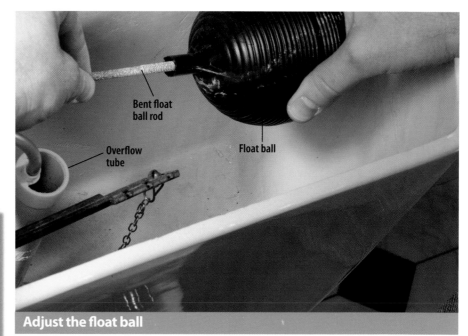

Bent float ball rod

Overflow tube

Float ball

Adjust the float ball

Remove the tank lid and check the water level. It should not pass into the overflow tube. If water is running into the tank, it will stop when you lift the float ball. Bend the rod slightly downward to lower the float ball. With a float-cup ballcock like the one shown on the opposite page, adjust the clip.

Flapper

Flush valve seat

Fix a leaky flush valve seat

If water continually trickles into the bowl and occasionally causes the toilet to flush weakly, the problem is probably in the flush valve. A flush valve has two parts: a flapper or a tank ball and the flush valve seat into which the flapper or ball drops to seal the bottom of the tank while it fills. Often the problem is a dirty seat.

Shut off the water to the tank and flush the toilet to get the water out.

Check the flapper or tank ball. If it has gunk on it, wipe it clean and smooth, using an abrasive pad. Once it's cleaned, feel the valve seat to see if it is pitted (or corroded if it's metal). Pry out and replace a damaged flexible seat. If the damaged seat is metal, replace the entire flush valve.

Bonnet

Diaphragm

Repair a diaphragm ballcock

Shut off the water and flush the toilet. Remove the four screws on top of the ballcock and lift off the bonnet. Clean out deposits. Replace worn parts, including the diaphragm. If several parts look worn, replace the entire ballcock.

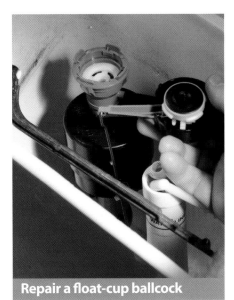

Repair a plunger ballcock

Shut off the water and flush the toilet. This is the oldest type of ballcock, and it has many parts that can go bad. You may need to replace it with either a diaphragm or float-cup ballcock, but first try cleaning and replacing the washers (doing so might solve the problem). Remove the thumbscrews holding the float rod

mechanism in place, then lift it out and set it aside. Pull up on the plunger to remove it. Typically you'll find a seat washer as well as a couple of other washers. In very old models, you may find leather washers. Remove and replace all of the washers, reassemble the mechanism, and turn on the water.

Repair a float-cup ballcock

Shut off the water and flush the toilet. This is the newest and the simplest design, and it rarely causes trouble. Pry off the cap. To remove the bonnet, lift the lever on the float rod mechanism, pushing the mechanism down and twisting counterclockwise. Clean out gunk and replace the seal if it looks worn.

TOILET REPAIR CHART

Symptom	Cause	Repair
Water continuously trickles or runs into tank and/or bowl (tank run-on).	Water level is too high.	Adjust trip lever chain, adjust water level in tank, or replace leaky float (see page 36).
	Flapper or tank ball seals improperly.	Clean the flush valve under the flapper, or replace worn flapper.
	Ballcock is faulty.	Repair or replace ballcock.
Bowl overflows when flushed. Toilet flushes incompletely.	Trap or drain is partially clogged.	Run a toilet auger through the toilet (see page 53), or clear the drain (see page 54).
	Trap or bowl is clogged.	
Tank leaks.	Water sprays up against the lid.	Anchor the refill tube so it sprays into the overflow tube.
	Gasket between tank and bowl is faulty.	Replace the spud gasket.
	Tank is cracked.	Replace the tank.
Bowl leaks. Leak appears as a wet spot on the floor.	Wax ring is not sealing.	Pull up the toilet and replace the wax ring (see page 38).
	Bowl is cracked.	Replace the bowl.
Tank sweats—drops of water appear on the outside.	Condensation occurs due to temperature difference between air and tank water.	Buy an insulation kit and install it inside the tank (page 39).

Fixing leaky tanks and bowls

- **TIME:** About 2 hours to replace a spud gasket or wax ring
- **SKILLS:** No special skills, but be careful not to crack the toilet
- **TOOLS:** Wrenches, screwdriver, putty knife

A puddle of water on the floor near the toilet may be the result of condensation or it may be a leak. On a hot, humid day, condensation from the cool outside of the tank or bowl may make a puddle. To rid yourself of the problem, install rigid-foam tank insulation (opposite page).

A chronic leak points to a faulty water supply connection, spud gasket, or wax ring. Tightening the hold-down bolts might solve the problem. Or, if there's a crack in the tank, patch it from the inside with silicone sealant. A cracked bowl should be replaced.

OLDER CONNECTIONS

With some older toilets, the tank connects to the bowl with a fitting. If leaks develop at either end of the fitting, tighten the nuts. If the leak persists, take the toilet apart and replace worn parts.

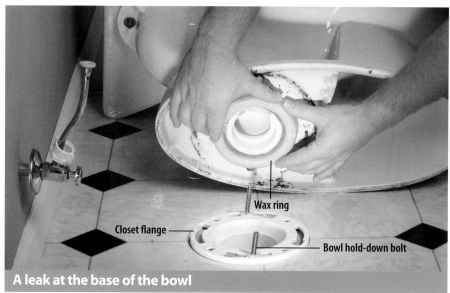

A leak at the base of the bowl

Wax ring

Closet flange

Bowl hold-down bolt

If the bowl is cracked, you'll have to replace it. If the bowl is sound, gently tighten the hold-down bolts. If that doesn't stop the leak, replace the wax ring. Shut off the water, flush the toilet, and sponge out remaining water. Disconnect the water supply line and remove the nuts on the hold-down bolts. Lift out the toilet. Scrape away the old wax ring and old putty on the bottom of the bowl. Press a new wax ring in place according to the manufacturer's directions. Reinstall the toilet (see pages 96–97).

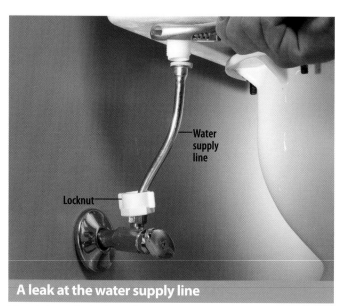

Water supply line

Locknut

A leak at the water supply line

First tighten the locknut that connects the water supply line. If that doesn't work, shut off the water, flush the toilet, and sponge out the water that remains in the tank. Disconnect the water supply line, remove the locknut, and replace the old beveled gasket and rubber washer with new ones.

Tank hold-down bolt

A leak between the tank and bowl

The tank hold-down bolts can loosen and produce a leak at the spud gasket. Use a screwdriver and a wrench to tighten the bolts. Do not overtighten; doing so can crack the tank. If the leak persists, you probably need to replace the gasket. Shut off the water, flush the toilet, and sponge out the tank. Detach the supply line, remove the bolts, lift off the tank, and replace the spud gasket (see pages 96–97).

Fixing a sweating tank

- **TIME:** About 20 minutes to 1 hour
- **SKILLS:** Measuring, cutting, applying mastic
- **TOOLS:** Pencil, straightedge, scissors, utility knife

Condensation can form on the outside of the toilet tank and drip onto the floor. Insulating the tank usually solves the condensation problem. You can buy a kit from your local home center or hardware store to insulate the tank and stop it from sweating, or you can purchase the materials and do the job yourself. Before you dive into the project, plan ahead. You will not be able to use the toilet overnight while the mastic dries.

HOT, HUMID AIR CAUSES SWEATING

When warm, humid air contacts the toilet tank, made cool by the cold water inside, moisture condenses on the tank. It's a common summer problem, but can happen even in the winter after running a hot shower.

1 Gather the materials

Gather your materials, including polystyrene foam. Next find the shutoff valve to the toilet. You'll typically find a shutoff below the tank and behind the bowl. Turn the valve to the closed position. If there is no stop valve, you'll need to shut the water off at the main shutoff (see page 14). Since the water will be off and you will be working in the area, now is a good time to install a stop valve for future repairs (see page 90). Remove all the water from the tank. Use a sponge and bucket to begin; use a towel to dry the tank.

2 Create a template

Place a piece of paper over the inside of one of the tank walls. The paper should be large enough to completely cover one side. Mark the edges of the wall with a pencil. Remove the paper and redraw the lines with a straightedge. Cut along the lines to create the template. Repeat this process for the other tank walls.

Using your template, cut out each piece of foam insulating sheet. Secure the template to the foam so you get a precise cut. You want to create a tight fit so water will not seep behind the foam pieces.

3 Apply mastic to back of sheet

Apply a bead of waterproof mastic to one side of a foam insulating sheet. Press the panel into place against the back wall of the tank. Repeat the process for the front and each side of the tank. Let the mastic dry overnight before refilling the tank.

Maintaining and repairing water heaters

- **TIME:** Allow 2 hours for inspection and minor repairs
- **SKILLS:** No special skills needed
- **TOOLS:** Adjustable wrench, groove-joint pliers

Water heaters are little more than giant insulated water bottles with heating elements inside. As hot water is used, cold water enters through a dip tube. This lowers the water temperature inside the tank, causing a thermostat to call for heat. In gas units, burners beneath the water tank kick in and continue heating the water until the desired temperature is reached. Heating elements perform the same function in electric water heaters.

Most water heater problems are the result of sediment buildup or rust. To help prevent this problem, open the drain valve every few months and flush out a few gallons of water. This purges rust and other buildup from the heater.

VITAL STATISTICS

The nameplate on the outside of your water heater also lists the unit's vital statistics. Look for:

- Tank Capacity: The more gallons it holds, the less chance you'll run out of hot water during a shower. A 40-gallon tank suits most households.
- R-Value: The better insulated the unit, the more efficient it will be. If yours has an R-value of less than seven, wrap the tank with insulation.
- Installation Clearances: This tells you how much room you must leave between the unit and any combustible materials.

GAS WATER HEATER

Cold water inlet
Flue
Dip tube
Gas control
Burner
Pilot
Thermocouple
Hot water outlet
Temperature-and-pressure-relief valve
Outer shell
Tank
Insulation
Drain valve

ELECTRIC WATER HEATER

Cold water inlet
Temperature-and-pressure-relief valve
Anode rod (attracts materials that otherwise would corrode the tank)
Upper heating element
Dip tube
Lower heating element
Drain valve
Electrical supply
Hot water outlet
Tank
Upper thermostat
Insulation
Access cover
Lower thermostat

WATER HEATER REPAIR CHART

Symptom	Cause	Repair
No hot water.	No power to the heater (electric). Pilot light out (gas).	Check circuit breaker or fuse (electric). Relight pilot; replace thermocouple if pilot does not stay lit (gas).
Water not hot enough.	Upper element burned out (electric).	Replace upper element (electric).
Not enough hot water, or hot water runs out quickly.	Thermostat set too low. Hot water must travel a long way to get to faucets. Sediment buildup in tank. Lower element burned out (electric). Dirt blocking burner (gas). Leaking faucets. Tank not large enough for demand.	Turn up thermostat. Insulate hot-water pipes (see page 58). Drain and refill tank. Replace lower element (electric). Clean burner, or call gas company (gas). Repair faucets. Replace with a larger tank.
Tank makes noise.	Sediment in tank.	Drain and refill tank.
Leak from temperature-and-pressure-relief valve.	Thermostat set too high. Defective relief valve.	Lower thermostat setting. Replace valve.
Leak around tank base.	Tank corrosion created a leak.	Replace water heater.

Replace a leaking drain valve

If your water heater's drain valve leaks, shut off the cold water stop valve, shut off the gas or the electrical current, and drain the water heater. Unscrew the faulty valve. Apply plumber's tape or pipe joint compound to the male threads of a new valve and install. Fill tank and restore power or gas.

Test the relief valve

Either on top or high on the side of the water heater, you'll find a relief valve (also called a T-and-P-relief valve) that opens if the temperature or pressure in the tank gets too high. Test it once a year: Pull on the handle; if water rushes out of the pipe attached to it, all is well.

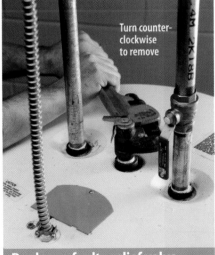

Replace a faulty relief valve

If no water comes out, replace the relief valve. Shut off the cold water, turn off power or gas to the unit, and drain some of the water. Remove the attached drainpipe and the valve. Apply plumber's tape or pipe joint compound to the male threads when you install the new valve.

Replacing an electric water heater thermostat

- **TIME:** About 2 hours
- **SKILLS:** Making electrical connections
- **TOOLS:** Screwdriver, voltage tester

If hot water is scarce at your house, make sure the water heater's thermostat is set correctly. Drain the heater if you suspect it is filled with sediment. If you have no hot water, check the unit for power. If none of these measures solves the problem, you may need to replace the thermostats and/or heating elements. Take the element and the thermostat to a plumbing supply house or an appliance repair shop for testing. Then follow the steps here to replace what is faulty.

Electric water heaters have two thermostats and two heating elements (see page 40). To find out which pair is defective, turn on a hot water faucet. If the water gets warm but not hot, the upper thermostat and element must be replaced. If the water is hot for a short while, then goes cold, replace the lower element and thermostat.

CAUTION

DANGER! HIGH VOLTAGE!
Electric water heaters use 240-volt current, twice the voltage found in standard receptacles. Be sure to remove the fuse or shut off the breaker at the service panel. Test wires for electricity before starting any work. A 240-volt circuit will likely have two fuses or a tandem circuit breaker.

1 Check for power

Shut off the power. Go to the main panel and turn off the circuit for the water heater. If you haven't labeled your breaker box, the circuit for an electric water heater is most likely on a 30-amp breaker. Shut off all the 30-amp breakers until you find the heater switch. Label it. Remove the screws from the heater access panel. Lift off the panel. Remove any insulation in the panel. Check for voltage using a voltage tester.

2 Remove the thermostat

Before disconnecting all the thermostat wires, label them. This will help you reconnect the proper wire to the correct terminal of the new thermostat. Disconnect the wires from the old thermostat. Remove the mounting clip and lift it out. Always replace an old thermostat with a new thermostat of the same model.

3 Install the new thermostat

To hook up the new thermostat, attach the mounting clip. Reconnect the wires to the terminals using your labels as a guide.

4 Reset the power

Read the manufacturer's instructions for the recommended temperature setting. Set the temperature. Make sure the tank is full. Turn the power back on at the circuit breaker. Press the red reset button on the thermostat. Replace insulation and reinstall the access panel.

Replacing an electric water heater element

- **TIME:** About 2 hours
- **SKILLS:** Making electrical connections
- **TOOLS:** Screwdriver, groove-joint pliers or element wrench, voltage tester

Take no chances: Turn off the circuit breaker to the water heater and test to make sure power is off (see page 42).

In most cases, two shutoff valves are located just above the tank. Turn them both off to keep water from flowing into the tank from either direction.

Once the repair has been made, loosened sediment will travel through the pipes and clog faucet aerators. Remove and clean the aerators for all the faucets; also clean the showerheads.

1 Drain the tank

Connect a hose to the water heater drain and run the other end to a nearby floor drain or a bucket. Open the water heater drain valve and let the water run completely out. Shut the valve off and disconnect the hose.

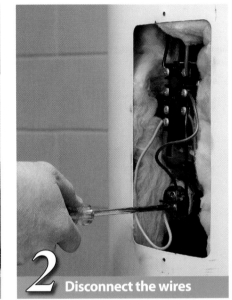

2 Disconnect the wires

Open the access panel. Loosen the terminal screws on the element and gently pull the wires away. If the bare wires are cracked, cut away the bare wire and restrip the insulation. There is no need to label the wires; they can connect to either terminal.

3 Remove the element

Unscrew and remove the element. An element wrench makes the task easy, but you can also use an adjustable wrench or channel-type pliers.

4 Replace the element

Buy an exact replacement element, with the same voltage and wattage ratings as the old element. Coat the new gasket with heat-resistant silicone grease. Slide the gasket over the heating element and seat it against the base. Screw the new element into the tank and tighten. Open both shutoff valves above the water heater until you hear the water flow stop. At each faucet in the house, remove the aerator. Turn on each faucet, allow the water to run for a minute to flush out debris, then shut it off. At the water heater, hook up the wires and tighten the terminal screws. Restore power to the water heater, press the reset button, and wait 20 minutes or so for the water to heat up. Run water in the faucets to test that the water is hot, then replace the aerators.

Repairing a gas water heater

■ **TIME:** 1 to 2 hours for any of the operations on these pages

■ **SKILLS:** Handling compression fittings on gas tubes

■ **TOOLS:** Wrench or pliers, thin wire, small wire brush, vacuum cleaner

If you suddenly lose hot water, or if your unit is not heating water efficiently, remove the access panel at the bottom of your water heater and check the pilot light. If it's not burning, relight it according to directions printed on the unit. If it won't relight, you need a new thermocouple. If a yellow rather than blue flame burns, you need to replace the thermocouple and/or clean the burner. If you smell smoke or fumes, check the flue immediately.

REGULAR MAINTENANCE FOR YOUR GAS WATER HEATER

To avoid the dangerous buildup of fumes from a faulty flue, check your flue at least once a year. Be sure it efficiently pulls fumes out of your house. To test, place a lit match near the flue. It should draw the flame up. If not, remove the flue and check for blockage. If none, call your local utility for assistance. An improperly working flue allows carbon monoxide into the house, so turn off the gas supply and electric power and open some windows to bring fresh air into the house.

Once a year, or at least whenever you replace the thermocouple, clean the burner. A clean burner operates more efficiently and extends the life of the water heater.

Gas control knob

1 Shut off gas to the water heater

At the control box, turn the top knob to the "off" position, and allow five minutes for gas in the lines to dissipate.

2 Disconnect tubes

Disconnect the three tubes that connect the burner to the control box using an adjustable wrench.

3 Remove the burner

Remove the burner access panel. Take care not to kink any of the tubes as you slide out the burner.

4 Clean and reinstall the burner

Clean the ports on the burner with brushes or a vacuum cleaner. Brush off loose rust. Slide the burner into the water heater. The flat end of the burner tube will fit securely into a slot in the bracket. Coil the excess thermocouple tubing in a loop 2 inches or larger. Take care not to kink the tubing. Align the tubes and connect them to the control using an adjustable wrench.

5 Relight the pilot

To relight the pilot, turn the control knob to the "pilot" position. Hold down the pilot button as you extend a fireplace match or a barbecue igniter to light the pilot. Keep the button depressed for at least 45 seconds, then release. The pilot should stay lit; if not, you may need to adjust the thermocouple's position. Turn the control knob to "on." The burners should ignite.

Replacing the thermocouple

If your pilot light fails to light or does not stay lit, replace the old thermocouple—a thin copper tube with a nut at one end and a solid tip at the other. Its tip may be simply pushed into a fitting, or it may be attached with a nut. Pull the thermocouple out of the bracket. At a home center or hardware store, buy an exact replacement.

Push the new thermocouple's tip into place until it seats firmly; tighten the nut, if there is one. The tip should be right next to the end of the pilot gas tube.

Return the burner unit and light the pilot (see Steps 4 and 5). The thermocouple's tip should touch the pilot flame; if not, adjust its position.

Opening clogged drains

Sooner or later, every homeowner encounters a clogged drain. If you hire a professional to clear it out, you will get a better price if you call someone who specializes in clearing drains rather than a general plumber. But it will still cost you plenty; a professional's time costs the same whether the job requires something highly specialized or is something you could have done yourself.

Most clogs are due to the slow buildup of solids that sink drains aren't intended to take. Only toilets are plumbed to handle solid waste; sinks, tubs, and showers have drains designed to carry away water only. Hair, grease, soap, food scraps, and gunk gradually clog a drain. With a few basic tools, you can clear most clogs and get the system flowing again.

POWER AUGERS

For extra augering power, rent or buy a power auger or an augering attachment for an electric drill. The drill attachment is less expensive but less sturdy than a power auger.

High-quality augers have a second cable that runs through the middle of the wound-wire augering cable. This keeps the auger cable from kinking, and it retrieves the auger cable if it should break. If your auger lacks this second cable and it breaks—a real possibility, especially if you are doing heavy-duty augering—you could end up with a length of auger cable stuck in your pipe.

ANATOMY OF A SINK

Lift rod

Pop-up assembly

Pivot rod

Blockage

Water in trap blocks sewer gas

Drainpipe

Trap

Blockage

Blockage

Where clogs happen

The slow buildup of soapy slime inside a drainpipe—usually at a point of resistance such as a drain assembly or a sharp bend in the drain—can cause a clog. If a fixture clogs often, install a strainer to keep solids from going down the drain. You'll have to clean the strainer occasionally, but it'll be worth it.

USING DRAIN CLEANERS

If your drain is completely stopped up and water is not moving through it at all, do not use a chemical drain cleaner. It will not help the problem, and some types will actually harden if they cannot get through, making the clog worse. Drain cleaner can damage pipes, and it might splash you when you plunge or auger the drain, injuring your skin or eyes.

If your drain is sluggish, use only nonacid drain cleaners (sodium hydroxide and copper sulfide). Wear long sleeves, gloves, and eye protection. Regular use of a drain cleaner keeps the pipes clear of hair, soap, grease, and so on.

To maintain a smooth-flowing drain, every week or so run very hot water into the drain for a minute or two. This will clear away small amounts of grease and soap and keep them from building up.

Unclogging methods

- **TIME:** 1 to 2 hours to perform the operations shown here
- **SKILLS:** No special skills needed
- **TOOLS:** Screwdriver, auger, plunger

The first step in clearing a sink clog is to figure out where the blockage might be. It could be anywhere along the three main sections of a household drain system: in the fixture drain; in the drain stack, which serves multiple fixtures; or in the main sewer line, which carries waste out of the house (see page 8). Usually the problem occurs close to a fixture, because the drainpipe and trap near a fixture are narrower than the stack and main sewer lines. Check other drains in your home. If more than one is clogged, something is probably stuck in a drain stack. If all drains are clogged, the problem is farther down the line, probably in the main sewer line.

PLUNGING SINKS WITH MORE THAN ONE DRAIN

Plunging a double sink requires a helper. Have him or her press a wet rag firmly into one of the drain holes while you plunge the other drain hole. A dishwasher drains through a hose into the disposer or the sink plumbing (see page 104). Before plunging, use a C-clamp and two wood blocks to seal the drain hose and keep water from backing into the dishwasher.

1 Clean the strainer

Sometimes clearing a sink is as easy as removing the strainer or stopper from the drain opening. Pull the stopper up and clear away soap, hair, food, or other debris that clogs the opening or dangles into the drain.

2 Detach the pop-up assembly

The strainers in kitchen sinks and some bathroom sinks lift out. Others require a slight turn before they lift out. With some, you must pull out the pivot rod before the stopper will come out. If you want to auger the sink, you will have to remove the pivot rod (see below).

3 Plunge a sink

A plunger uses water pressure to push out obstructions and suction to bring them up. The plunger's rubber cup must seal tightly around the drain opening. Water in the sink helps create a seal; petroleum jelly around the plunger rim also helps. Stuff a rag into any openings, such as the overflow drain, then push and pull rapidly with the plunger.

4 Auger a sink

If plunging fails, fit an auger down the drain. Cranking the auger handle rotates a stiff spring that bores through stubborn blockages. The auger may push a blockage through, or it may snag a blockage and pull it up and out. If none of these techniques works, see pages 48–49.

Augering techniques

■ **TIME:** Approximately 1 to 2 hours
■ **SKILLS:** Basic plumbing skills
■ **TOOLS:** Hand auger, pliers, adjustable wrench, gloves, goggles

If the clog is too stubborn for a plunger, try a drain auger. You'll find two types: a closet auger, made to slide easily through the trap of a toilet (see page 53), and a drain auger, which may be a coiled rod or a flat, springy metal strip.

When using a drain auger, you can go through the drain or you can remove the trap (see opposite page), depending on where you believe the clog is located. It is often better to remove a sink trap rather than try to auger through it.

To use the auger, loosen the setscrew and push the auger into the drain or pipe. When you feel resistance, you are probably up against the clog. Pull an extra 6–8 inches of cable out of the housing, tighten the setscrew securing the cable, and turn the crank on the auger, applying moderate force as you push the auger into the drainpipe. Sometimes this is enough to clear the blockage. When the free cable has worked into the pipe, loosen the setscrew and pull out 6 to 8 inches more. Firmly move the snake back and forth until the blockage is freed. If you are working through the drain, pour water into the drain from a bucket as you work the auger.

When the blockage has been cleared, reassemble the trap and flush the line. Run additional water down the drain to make sure the blockage is gone. If water backs up, there may still be some debris in the line left behind by the auger. Try plunging to get rid of residual debris, then flush with hot water. Otherwise, the problem may be in the main drain or sewer line (see pages 54–55).

Tailpiece

Remove bend if possible

Setscrew

Trap

1 Set up a drop cloth and pan

Be prepared for a mess if you go in through the trap. Place a drop cloth and a dishpan below the drain opening and wear gloves. Remove the trap and elbow as well as the pipe that leads to the wall. Loosen the setscrew of the auger and push the auger cable into the drainpipe until you feel it meet resistance.

Extend 6 to 8 inches of cable from the housing to work with and tighten the setscrew. Crank the auger handle clockwise, pushing it in until the auger moves forward. Once it is past an obstruction like a bend in the pipe, you may be able to push the cable in without cranking it.

2 Push and pull

Augers can pass through soft obstructions such as soap clogs: Use a push-and-pull motion to ream them out. If the auger comes to an obstruction and it will not crank easily, pull it out. Often the blockage will come out with it. Sometimes the auger clears the line by pushing the blockage through to a larger pipe.

CAUTION

WORK SLOWLY AND CAREFULLY
Use care while feeding the auger cable into the drain. It is possible to push the trap apart or damage it if you push the auger too hard.

CAUTION

PROTECT YOURSELF FROM CHEMICALS
Always use gloves and goggles to avoid skin contact with bacteria and chemical drain cleaners. Cleaners burn skin and damage eyes. Don't use a chemical drain cleaner before using mechanical methods.

SELECTING AN AUGER

Drain augers are useful when a clog is too much to clear with plunging alone. The best auger is a coiled cable that wraps inside a housing. The housing should have a handle and a crank on it for spinning the cable inside the drain.

PREVENTIVE MAINTENANCE

The bathroom sink needs a good flushing to clear buildup of hair and grease. Boil some water and pour it down the sink. Boiled water is much hotter than tap water and will dissolve sludge coating the walls of your drainpipes. Do this once every two months or so and you'll avoid most clogs.

Dismantling a fixture trap

- **TIME:** About 1 hour to dismantle and reassemble a trap
- **SKILLS:** Beginner plumbing skills
- **TOOLS:** Groove-joint pliers, joint tape or pipe joint compound

When plunging doesn't clear a clog or if you've dropped something valuable into a drain, you may have to dismantle the trap. Before you take it apart, however, see if the trap has a nutlike cleanout fitting at its lowest point. If it does, open it and see if you can clear the clog or retrieve the item with a stiff wire through the hole.

If there is no cleanout, don't be discouraged. Dismantling a trap is not particularly difficult or time-consuming. The most difficult part of the job is getting a wrench into position if the trap is in an awkward place.

1 Open and drain the trap

Turn off the faucet firmly. As an extra precaution, turn off the supply valves. Position a bucket to catch the water that will spill out when you remove the trap. Loosen the slip nuts that secure the trap.

Wrap electrical tape around the jaws of your wrench or pliers to protect the nuts from scratches. After a half-turn or so, you can unscrew the nuts by hand.

2 Disassemble the trap

The joints of the trap are made up of a nut and a flexible washer. Push them up the tailpiece and elbow to keep track of them. Dump out the water that sits in the trap.

3 Clean out the trap

Remove any gunk that has collected. Clean the inside of the trap with a small wire brush or run a piece of cloth through it. Replace washers that show signs of wear and slide the trap back into position.

4 Reassemble

Wrap the male threads with joint tape or brush on joint compound. Position trap, slide washers into place, and hand-tighten the slip nuts. Use an adjustable wrench for final tightening. To test for leaks, fill the sink, then remove the plug. Tighten the slip nut if necessary.

Unclogging a shower

■ **TIME:** 2 hours to try both methods
■ **SKILLS:** Basic plumbing skills
■ **TOOLS:** Auger, screwdriver, garden hose attached to a spout, rags

If a shower stall drains sluggishly, carefully pour 1 to 3 gallons of boiling water down the drain or run the hot water for about 10 minutes. Hot water works on the elements (soap and grease) that bind a blockage.

If hot water fails, try plunging, then use an environmentally safe chemical drain cleaner. Do not use chemical cleaners on completely stopped drains.

The most effective chemical cleaners are either acidic or caustic; both can harm you. Read the label carefully and follow all safety precautions and the manufacturer's instructions for use.

If a shower drain is clogged, fill the base with an inch of water and plunge. If the drain does not respond to plunging, use a screwdriver to pry up the strainer and attempt to clear the blockage with the two methods shown here. (Some strainers have a center screw; remove it first.)

1 Run an auger

Push an auger down the drain and through the trap. Push and pull to remove a soap clog. If the auger hits a blockage, pull out the auger. The blockage may come with it. If it doesn't, use the auger to force the clog into a larger pipe.

2 Push in a hose

If all else fails, try forcing out the blockage with a hose. Remove the strainer. Guide the hose in as far as it will easily go, and pack rags tightly around the hose at the drain opening. Hold everything in place and have a helper turn the water fully on and off a few times.

Unclogging a tub

■ **TIME:** 2 hours to try both methods
■ **SKILLS:** Basic plumbing skills
■ **TOOLS:** Plunger, auger, screwdriver

If a bathtub drains sluggishly but is not stopped, pour 1 to 3 gallons of boiling water down the drain or run the hot water for about 10 minutes.

If hot water alone doesn't work, try plunging. Then use an environmentally safe chemical drain cleaner. The most effective chemical cleaners are either acidic or caustic; both can harm you. Read the label carefully and follow all safety precautions and the manufacturer's instructions for use.

If the stubborn blockage refuses to clear, remove the strainer and work an auger through the drain. If you're still unable to remove or reach the blockage, work through the overflow drain.

Pop-up stopper

1 Try plunging first

If your tub has a pop-up stopper, remove it before you plunge. Wiggle it to free the linkage assembly—the mechanism that connects the trip lever with the stopper mechanism. Before plunging, plug the overflow and run an inch or so of water into the tub to help seal the plunger.

2 Auger through the drain

If plunging fails, thread an auger through the drain. Remove the stopper and/or the trip-lever linkage. Insert the auger into the opening. This method reaches only to the T-fitting. If the clog is farther down the drain, you'll have to put the auger through the overflow tube.

3 Auger through the overflow

Remove the pop-up or trip-lever assembly by unscrewing the plate and pulling out the parts (see page 60). Feed the auger down the overflow tube and through the trap. If the auger goes in a long way and the stoppage remains, find a clean-out plug on the main drain and auger there.

Unclogging a sink

■ **TIME:** 1 to 2 hours
■ **SKILLS:** Basic plumbing skills
■ **TOOLS:** Plunger, auger, screwdriver, pipe wrenches, bucket, rags

To clear a sink drain, you'll need only a few basic tools. Addressing it yourself saves the expense of hiring a plumber. Just acknowledge your limitations and don't be too aggressive. You don't want to damage the drainpipe by applying too much force.

Most sink clogs happen in bathrooms. Kitchen and laundry sinks do not normally clog—hot water from dishwashers and clothes washers purges them by removing grease and sludge. Bathroom sinks clog because of constant exposure to hair, soap, and greasy products.

Avoid reaching for a chemical product to clear a blockage. Chemical products are great for maintenance when used in moderation; but when a blockage occurs, chemical products can create more harm than good and pose a safety hazard. The caustic chemicals can actually damage the pipes. The best way to unclog a drain is mechanically.

Try carefully pouring 1 to 3 gallons of boiling water down the drain. Extremely hot water works to release the blockage by working on the elements that bind a blockage—soap and grease.

Make sure there is water in the sink

Once a clog has formed, preventive measures will not work. It is time to get out the plunger. Partially fill the sink with water to cover the plunger head. If you have a double sink or an overflow opening, stuff a wet rag into the second drain or opening. This will focus the plunging pressure on the clog. Now plunge up and down vigorously, keeping the plunger sealed against the bottom of the sink. If you do not feel the water swishing back and forth or enough resistance, then air may be escaping through the second drain or overflow opening. Have a helper hold the wet rag firmly in place. Once you have broken the clog loose, run hot water through the drain to flush out the debris.

Unclog kitchen sinks

If the sink has a double bowl, plug one side with a wet cloth and hold it firmly in place. Run hot water into the sink, the hotter the better. If the obstruction doesn't clear, try plunging. Take care that the plug on the other side of the double bowl doesn't come loose. Apply a thick layer of petroleum jelly to the rim of the plunger to create a tight seal before using it.

If this fails, run a snake through the trap under the sink. Check the trap for a clean-out plug. If it has one, carefully remove it after placing a bucket under it first, as water will run out.

The trap is held in place by a slip nut on each end. Remove the slip nuts with a pipe wrench. Once the trap is removed, check to see if it's clogged. If the blockage is inside the trap, push an old bottle brush around the bends of the trap to remove debris. Feed an auger into the drainpipe, if the trap is clear. You should eventually run into some resistance. Turn the auger, feed another foot or two into the pipe, then pull it out. There should be some debris on the tip of the snake. Reassemble the trap and try running hot water through the pipe. If still clogged, try plunging again. You may need to repeat the whole process once or twice.

Unclogging a toilet

■ **TIME:** 1 to 2 hours
■ **SKILLS:** Basic plumbing skills
■ **TOOLS:** Plunger, closet auger, screwdriver, pipe wrenches, bucket, rags

Do not continue to flush a clogged toilet. Flushing will not push objects through and will more likely flood the bathroom floor. Instead bail out the toilet until the bowl is about half full. The plunger needs some water to make a tight seal around the bowl. Most toilet clogs occur because the toilet trap is blocked. If a plunger or toilet auger fails to clear things up, the waste-vent stack may be blocked.

CAUTION

NO CHEMICALS ALLOWED

Never attempt to unclog a toilet with a chemical drain cleaner. Chances are it won't do the job, and you'll be forced to plunge or auger through a strong solution that could splash and burn your skin or eyes.

HOW TO STOP A TOILET OVERFLOW

If the toilet bowl begins to overflow, act quickly. Remove everything on top of the tank and lift off the lid. Pull the float up and push down on the flapper valve at the tank bottom. The flush will stop.

Plunge the toilet with force

An ordinary plunger can clear a toilet, but the molded-cup type generates stronger suction. Work up and down vigorously for about a dozen strokes, then quickly yank away the plunger.

If the water disappears with a glug, it's likely the plunging has succeeded—but don't flush yet. Pour in more water and empty the bowl as before several times. If plunging doesn't work, auger the toilet.

The auger's plastic cover protects the toilet

Use a closet auger

A closet auger makes short work of most toilet stoppages. This specialized tool has a long handle with a plastic cover at the bend to protect your toilet from scratches. To operate it, pull the spring all the way up into the handle (it will barely protrude from the plastic protective cover on the end of the auger). Insert the bit into the bowl outlet and crank. If you meet resistance, pull back slightly, wiggle the handle, and try again. A closet auger can grab and pull many blockages, but not solid objects such as toys. If you hear something other than the auger rattling around, remove the toilet to get at the item (see page 96).

Clearing main drains and sewer lines

- **TIME:** 1 to 2 hours
- **SKILLS:** Basic plumbing skills
- **TOOLS:** Plunger, auger, screwdriver, pipe wrenches, bucket, rags

Some objects defy ordinary removal techniques. Many of these clogs result when a small child places a toy in the toilet. No matter what you try, you can't pull the object back out. The answer may be to push or flush the object into a larger, downstream drainpipe. Then dislodge and remove the object at a cleanout or trap. Just be aware that pushing a blockage downstream may require hiring a plumber to remove it, especially if there are no downstream traps or cleanouts.

Start with the highest cleanout you can find that is below the clogged fixture. If augering it does not work, continue working downward. An option is to go on the roof and run an auger through the vent stack. This job often warrants calling in a plumber or a drain-cleaning service, especially if the line is clogged with tree roots.

Practice preventive maintenance to avoid future clogs. Flush the drains once a week with hot tap water. This helps clear out residual soap, grease, and debris that enter the drainpipes with normal use. Clean drains once every six months using a nonacidic drain cleaner. Acidic cleaners can harm pipes.

Auger a cleanout

Look for a cleanout near the bottom of your home's soil stack. Loosen the plug of the cleanout. If water flows out, the blockage is below. (If no water flows out, the blockage may be holding the water above, so replace the clean-out plug and auger from a higher point.) Insert the auger and run it back and forth several times (see page 48).

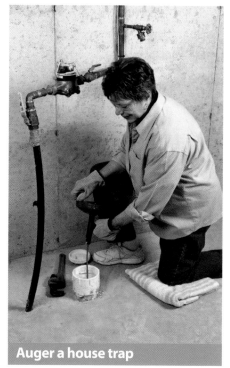

Auger a house trap

If neither procedure works, move farther down the line. Some houses have a trap near the place where the drain line exits the house. Open one of the two plugs and thread in an auger. The blockage may be in the trap itself.

CAUTION

GET YOUR PAIL READY

Before removing a cleanout plug from a main drain line, grab some buckets to catch the wastewater. Cover the floor near the plug with old towels and wrap towels around the pipe.

Use a blow bag

Another solution is to use a blow bag. Hook the blow bag up to a garden hose and connect it to a hose bib or utility faucet. Thread the blow bag and the hose into the drain. Turn on the water supply. Be patient. It may take several minutes. Blow bags are most effective for clearing blockages in floor drains.

Cleanout plugs

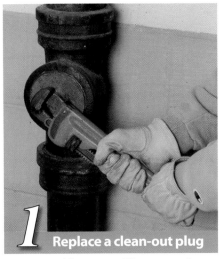

1 Replace a clean-out plug

Be prepared for a mess. When removing a drain plug, you don't know what you'll find. Have rags and a bucket in place. Remove the clean-out plug with a pipe wrench. If you can't get the plug to move, give it a squirt or two of penetrating oil. Stubborn plugs may require brute force. Place a chisel on the edge of the plug and strike it with a hammer. If this doesn't work, you may have to break the plug.

2 Install a plastic plug ...

The new plug will need a good seal. Coat the threads with pipe joint compound or wrap the threads with joint tape.

or install a rubber plug

If the threads in the pipe are damaged, use an expandable rubber plug to seal the opening. Place the plug in the opening. Turn the wing nut until the rubber expands to seal the opening.

Clean a sewer line

If the blockage remains, the outdoor sewer line may be the problem. Often fine tree roots work their way into the line, creating an obstacle that only a heavy auger with a cutting bit can remove. First try using a garden hose to flush out the obstruction. If that doesn't work, call in a professional or rent a heavy-duty power auger. Running a power auger is a two-person job. Get a demonstration from the rental center.

Clearing a drum trap

1 Open the drum trap

Many older bathrooms have a removable metal cap on the floor (usually near the tub), which covers a drum trap. Before removing the cap to open the trap, bail out the tub and remove standing water with rags or a large sponge.

2 Unclog a drum trap

Auger through the drum trap. You may have difficulty removing the cap. If a wrench doesn't do the trick, use a hammer and cold chisel or screwdriver. Damage the cap if necessary (you can replace it easily), but don't mar the threads on the trap. Open the trap slowly, watching for water to well up around the threads. If the trap is full, work the auger away from the tub toward the main drain. If the trap is only partially full (as shown), the obstruction is between the tub and the trap: Auger back and forth. Drum traps are no longer acceptable to code and must be replaced with a P-trap.

Fixing leaking and frozen pipes

■ **TIME:** About 1 hour to clamp or apply epoxy to a leak
■ **SKILLS:** No special skills needed
■ **TOOLS:** Screwdriver, putty knife, adjustable wrench, hammer, chisel

Water that escapes from a pipe can wreak havoc in your house. Even a tiny leak that is left to drip day and night soon rots away everything in its vicinity. A pipe that freezes and bursts can produce a major flood.

As soon as you spot any sign of a leak, shut off the water to take pressure off the line. Then locate exactly where the problem is. If the pipe is concealed, this may be difficult, because water can travel a long way on the outside of the pipe, a floor joist, or a subfloor. Eventually a leaking pipe must be replaced, but these emergency measures will temporarily stop the flow.

IT MAY NOT BE A LEAK

If a pipe appears wet all along its length, the problem may be condensation from humid air rather than leaking. Wrap the pipe with insulation to stop the condensation (see page 58).

OR IT MAY BE MORE

Sometimes an isolated leak signifies aging pipes. The galvanized pipe common to older homes tends to rust from the inside out. Once a leak appears, you can expect others to follow. If the pipes in your house have begun to deteriorate, buy a supply of pipe clamps to fit your lines.

Wrap with tape

For a pinhole leak, dry off the pipe and wrap it tightly with several layers of electrician's tape six inches on either side of the hole. This is a temporary solution. The tape should hold while you make a trip to the hardware store for a pipe clamp and rubber gasket.

Apply a clamp

Hose clamp

An automotive hose clamp with a piece of rubber—both available at hardware stores—is a better solution (for pinhole leaks only). Wrap the rubber around the pipe and tighten the clamp. Be sure you place the clamp directly over the hole.

Rubber gasket

1 To install a pipe clamp, position the gasket

The best temporary solution to a leaking pipe is a pipe clamp specially made for this purpose. A clamp seals small gashes, cracks, and pinhole leaks. As a semipermanent solution, it should last several years. Position the rubber gasket so the hole is centered under it.

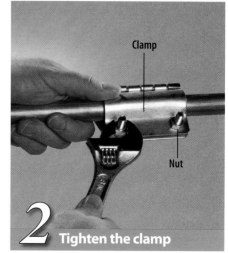

Clamp

Nut

2 Tighten the clamp

Assemble the clamp pieces around the gasket. Take care that the gasket does not move as you tighten all the nuts evenly, working from nut to nut until all are tight.

Apply plumber's epoxy at fittings

If the leak is coming from a fitting, don't try to clamp it. Plumber's epoxy is the best solution here. Unless the leak is a real gusher, don't shut off the water. The epoxy comes in two parts. Cut a piece of each and knead them together until the color is uniform. Pack the epoxy into the connection, pushing it in with your thumb or a putty knife. Pack it until the leak stops.

Seal a leaking cleanout

Drain lines are less leak-prone than supply lines. Once in a while, however, a cleanout plug seeps wastewater. If so, warn everyone in the household not to use any fixtures while you work. Remove the plug (it may screw out or pull out). To reseal a screw-in plug, apply pipe-thread tape to the male threads. If it has an O-ring, replace it.

Tighten joints in cast-iron pipes

Leaks that occur at the joint of cast-iron pipes are usually easy to deal with. For the hub fitting shown here, use a hammer and chisel to tamp down the soft lead that fills the joint. Don't whack the pipe: You could crack it. If your pipes are joined with no-hub connectors (see page 125), simply tighten the clamp to stop the leak.

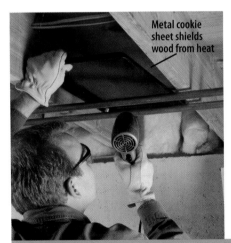

Metal cookie sheet shields wood from heat

To thaw exposed frozen pipes, heat with a blow dryer ...

Open the faucet the pipe supplies so steam can escape. If the pipe is exposed, apply heat directly with a hair dryer or a heat gun (use the lowest setting). Move the dryer or gun back and forth—don't hold it in one spot. Shield nearby wood from the heat.

or pour hot water

Another solution for an exposed frozen pipe is to wrap a cloth around it, then pour boiling water over the cloth. Allow the water on the cloth to cool, pour hot water again, and repeat until the pipe is thawed. Be sure a faucet is open while you do this so steam can escape.

Thaw concealed pipes

If the pipes are concealed, thawing takes more time. Open a faucet. Beam a heat lamp or electric space heater at the wall that contains the pipe. Monitor closely to make sure the heat doesn't damage the wall surface.

Preventing freeze-ups

■ **TIME:** About 3 hours to prepare the average home
■ **SKILLS:** Beginner maintenance and plumbing skills
■ **TOOLS:** Knife, flashlight

Ice-cold tap water may taste refreshing, but it also can be a chilling sign that your plumbing is in trouble. Frozen pipes that have burst are difficult and expensive to fix, so take precautions if you suspect that your system will not survive the coldest days of the year. Pipes that run near an exterior wall in new homes are as prone to freezing as pipes in poorly insulated older homes. Often the best solution is to insulate the wall or ceiling that contains the pipes, which helps keep a home warm and protects pipes at the same time. This page shows some additional ways to prevent freeze-ups.

Insulate the pipes

Insulation prevents freeze-ups, as long as every square inch of pipe—including connections—is protected. Pipe jacketing comes in standard lengths that can be cut with a knife and secured with electrical tape. Ordinary insulation, cut in strips and bundled around pipes, works equally well for less cost but more labor. For extremely cold walls or floors, pack the entire cavity with insulation. Also consider insulating long runs of hot-water pipes, especially those that pass through unheated spaces. The added insulation conserves energy used to heat the water.

Wrap pipes with heat tape

Electric heat tape draws modest amounts of current, so it is safe and inexpensive to use. Wrap tape around the pipe and plug the tape into a receptacle. A thermostat turns the tape on and off as needed. Tape will not work during a power outage—when the protection may be most needed.

Protect the sill cock

Before winter cold arrives, remove and drain garden hoses to prevent them from splitting. Shut off the water leading to the sill cock, allow it to drain, and leave it open. If there is no indoor shutoff, install one (see page 90) or install a freezeproof sill cock—an improvement that local codes may require.

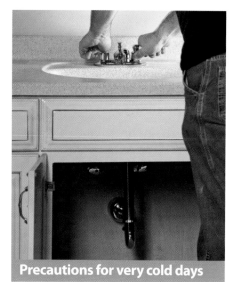

Precautions for very cold days

As a preventive measure on extremely cold days, slightly turn on the faucets that have vulnerable parts, letting water trickle constantly. If there is a cabinet underneath, open its doors to let room heat warm the pipes. Use a small lamp to warm pipes that run through cold areas such as a garage or closet.

Winterizing a house

■ **TIME:** About 4 hours to winterize an average-size house
■ **SKILLS:** Disconnecting pipes
■ **TOOLS:** Pipe wrench, adjustable wrench, bucket

If you're leaving a house or cabin for an extended period of time during the winter, you don't have to leave the heat on in order to avoid plumbing disasters. Instead, save money by turning off your utilities and winterizing them, a process that involves shutting off the water supply and draining the whole plumbing system. If you have a private water system, such as a well, the process is slightly more involved because you'll have to drain the holding tank and any water-treating apparatus. As a result, you'll have peace of mind that the plumbing system is safely dormant, without the expense of keeping the home fires burning.

HOME AGAIN

After returning to your winterized house, follow these steps, in order:

■ Turn all faucets off, including the sill cock. Remove any faucet aerators and clean if necessary.
■ Reconnect all disconnected pipes and close all drainable valves.
■ Turn on the valve for the main water supply.
■ Turn on all the faucets slowly, beginning at the sill cock. The water will spit out before resuming a normal flow.
■ Replace the aerators.

1 Drain the system

Have the water department shut off the water valve outside your home, or do it yourself. Then open every faucet in the house, starting at the top of the system. Shut down and drain the water heater (see Step 1, page 43). Detach drain hoses on dishwashers and clothes washers.

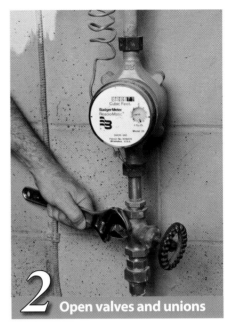

2 Open valves and unions

See if your system has a drainable valve or two—often they are near the water meter. Open the drain cock on each. Drain supply lines completely. If you find a low-lying pipe without a faucet or drain cock, open the line at a union where two pipes join (see page 80).

3 Replace water with antifreeze

Flush toilets, then pour a gallon of antifreeze solution (automotive antifreeze mixed with water according to directions on the container) into the bowl. This will start a mild flushing action, though some of it will remain in the toilet's trap.

Pour antifreeze solution into all fixtures with a trap: sinks, showers, bathtubs, and the washing machine standpipe. If your house has a main house trap, fill the elbow portion with full-strength antifreeze.

Adjusting drain assemblies

- **TIME:** 1 hour for most adjustments
- **SKILLS:** Basic plumbing skills
- **TOOLS:** Screwdriver, pliers

If the water in your bathroom sink or tub gradually leaks out even though you've stopped the drain, or if it doesn't drain out readily, you may need to adjust the drain assembly.

Before dismantling the assembly, pull up the strainer or stopper and remove any hair or other debris hanging from it. Thoroughly clean away soap or other gunk that may be keeping the strainer or stopper from seating properly.

Trip-lever drain

A trip lever lifts and lowers a seal plug at the base of the overflow tube. When the seal plug drops into its seat, water from the tub drain can't get past. But because the plug is hollow, water can still flow through the overflow tube.

Dismantle and adjust a trip lever as you would a tub pop-up unit. If the seal on the bottom of the plug is worn, replace it.

Pop-up drains

If you've cleaned out the strainer and stopper and the problem persists, check the stopper seal. If it's damaged, replace any rubber parts or replace the stopper itself. Look for signs of wear on the flange the stopper seats into.

On a bathroom sink, examine the pivot rod. When the stopper is closed, a working rod slants slightly up from the pivot to the clevis. If it doesn't, loosen the setscrew, raise or lower the clevis on the lift rod, and retighten the screw.

If the stopper doesn't operate as easily now as you would like, squeeze the spring clip, pull the pivot rod out of the clevis, and reinsert it into the next higher or lower hole. If water drips from the pivot, try tightening its cap. If the pivot still drips, you may need to replace the seal inside.

To adjust a tub pop-up, unscrew the overflow plate, withdraw the entire assembly, and loosen the adjusting nuts. If the stopper doesn't seat tightly, move the middle link higher on the striker rod. If the tub is slow to drain, lower the link.

Maintaining a garbage disposer

- **TIME:** Less than 1 hour to deal with most problems
- **SKILLS:** No special skills needed, unless you need to auger
- **TOOLS:** Allen wrench or disposer turning tool, flashlight, auger, broom handle

To avoid maintenance problems, be sure you have cold water running before you turn on your disposer. Gradually feed in food waste and don't stick a spatula or spoon past the splash guard. With the cold water continuing to flow, run the disposer for a few seconds after the food has been ground. A clanking sound usually means a utensil or some other item is caught in the disposer. Switch off or unplug the disposer and remove the object that has caused the problem.

CAUTION

DON'T USE CHEMICALS
Don't attempt to clear a blocked drain line with chemicals of any kind—not even "safe" chemicals. If the solution doesn't work, you'll be in danger of getting spattered with it when you try to clear the line.

Solve jams with a special turning tool

Your disposer may come with an allen wrench that fits into a hole at the bottom of the disposer. If not, you can purchase a tool like the one shown. In either case, use the tool to turn the disposer back and forth. Once it rotates freely, make sure it is switched off, remove the obstruction, replace the splash guard, turn on the cold water, and test the disposer.

Reset an overloaded disposer

If your disposer motor shuts off during operation, its overload protector has sensed overheating and has broken the electrical connection. Wait a few minutes for the unit to cool, then push the red reset button on the bottom of the disposer. If that doesn't work, check the power to the unit. Inspect the cord and the fuse or circuit breaker.

Disassemble and auger the drain

Because a disposer gobbles up huge amounts of food waste, you can expect the drain line to clog occasionally. If this happens, disassemble and remove the P-trap (make sure you have a bucket handy) and clean out the trap (see page 49). If the trap itself is clear, thread a drain auger into the drainpipe (see page 48).

REMOVE STUCK OBJECTS

If any solid object gets past the splash guard, it can cause the disposer to jam. If this happens, turn off the power (it may have shut itself off). Remove the splash guard and look into the disposer with a flashlight. If you can't free the object, rotate the grinder with a broom handle or turning tool.

Replacing a sink strainer

- **TIME:** About 2 hours to disassemble and reassemble a strainer
- **SKILLS:** Intermediate plumbing skills
- **TOOLS:** Adjustable wrench (and possibly a spud wrench), putty knife, plumber's putty, joint compound

A slight leak under the sink at the tailpiece is likely the result of a poor seal between the strainer body and the sink.

To check for this, plug the sink, fill the bowl, and look for drips.

If water drips from the place where the strainer body joins the sink, disassemble the strainer and apply new putty. Leaks also may occur where the tailpiece joins the strainer body. If so, tighten the slip nut. If that does not solve the problem, replace the washer.

Sink strainer parts

The sink strainer captures waste that otherwise would clog the drain. Its wide bowl is held snug against the sink bottom by the locknut. Putty and a rubber gasket sandwich the sink for a tight seal. The strainer body connects to the tailpiece with a washer and a slip nut.

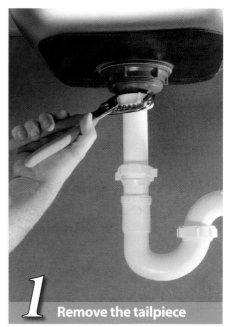

1 Remove the tailpiece

Use an adjustable wrench to loosen the slip nut beneath the strainer body and the slip nut above the trap bend. Unscrew it by hand, then remove the tailpiece.

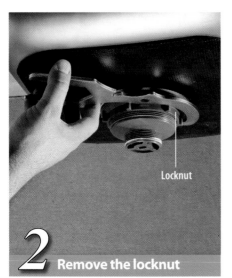

2 Remove the locknut

You may have difficulty removing the locknut, especially if it is hard to reach. Consider purchasing a spud wrench, which is specially designed to fit on locknuts. Or tap gently with a hammer and screwdriver to loosen the nut.

3 Remove old putty

Use a putty knife to scrape the old putty from the drain opening. Clean the opening thoroughly with a scouring pad soaked with paint thinner. If you plan to reuse the strainer, clean off the flange of the strainer as well.

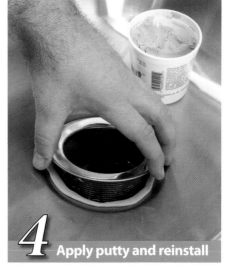

4 Apply putty and reinstall

Make a rope of putty and place it on the lip of the drain opening. Press the strainer into the opening. From under the sink, slip on the rubber gasket and the fiber washer; screw on the locknut. Tighten the locknut until the strainer nests completely into the sink. Reinstall the tailpiece.

TOOLS, MATERIALS, AND SKILLS

Essential tools

Plumbing does not require a lot of expensive tools, and some that you may use for only one job are well worth the cost. The money you save by doing your own work pays for them many times over. Using the tools shown on this page, you can tackle most plumbing projects.

Adjustable wrench
This wrench adjusts to fit the nuts on faucets and other fixtures. Cleanout plugs and drum traps often require an adjustable wrench.

Auger
A hand-cranked drain auger can clear away clogs that resist simple plunging.

Drill
For running new pipes through walls, you will need a drill and spade bits or hole saws of the correct size. You can use either a corded or cordless drill, but variable speed and reversing features are musts for drilling large holes through framing.

Closet auger
This auger is designed to clear toilets. The tube is bent to go up into the closet bend.

Flashlight
You'll often have to make plumbing repairs in dark places, such as under a sink or in a corner of the basement.

Groove-joint pliers
Use this tool to disassemble and connect pipes and to make myriad other plumbing repairs. The pliers adjust to grab various sizes of pipes and fittings.

Hacksaw
You can cut all kinds of pipe with a hacksaw. Blades dull quickly on steel, so have extra blades available.

Keyhole saw
This is a handy saw for cutting into drywall or plaster to make room for plumbing work.

Needle-nose pliers
You can remove O-rings or clips and reach into tight spots with needle-nose pliers.

Pipe wrench
A standard adjustable pipe wrench is essential for working with threaded iron pipe. It's usually best to have two of them—one to hold a pipe or fitting and one to turn the joining piece.

Plunger
This is the basic tool for clearing drain lines. This type, with the extra flange extending downward, is ideal for toilets and also works well on bathtubs and sinks.

Putty knife
A putty knife comes in handy for scraping off old sealants and for other uses.

Screwdrivers
Have a good selection of straight and phillips screwdrivers on hand for plumbing. Short ones are often handy.

Spade bits
To run new pipes, you'll need to drill holes 1 inch or larger through walls and framing. Spade bits are economical tools for making large holes.

Tape measure
Accurate measurements are a must for running new pipes or replacing old ones.

Utility knife
A knife often comes in handy when making plumbing repairs or installations.

Specialized tools

Some tools are designed for specialized plumbing tasks. Choose the ones that will most help you work with your materials and fixtures. Here are some you might need.

Basin wrench
When you can't reach a faucet nut with pliers or a wrench, this tool is the answer.

Blow bag
A blow bag might do the trick when plungers and augers can't clear out a clog. Hook it up to a garden hose, insert it into the drainpipe, and turn on the water.

Cold chisel
If you have to chip away concrete or tile to do your plumbing job, use a cold chisel.

Crimping tool
Make permanent connections in PEX tubing installations with this tool. The tool includes a gauge you can use to check the crimp.

Flaring tool
This forms the end of copper tubing to make flare-nut connections.

Level
Rely on a level to set drain lines to the correct slope.

Plastic tubing cutter
This tool cuts plastic supply tubes quickly and cleanly.

Propane torch
Soldering copper pipe requires a propane torch. If you have a lot to do, pay the extra money for one with a built-in lighter.

Reciprocating saw
For large-scale demolition, notching studs and joists, and quickly cutting galvanized pipe, a reciprocating saw is indispensable.

Seat wrench
This is the best tool to use to remove and replace seats in faucets that have washers.

Spark lighter
Always use a spark lighter instead of matches to light a propane torch.

Spud wrench
You might need this for the big nut that secures the strainer body in a kitchen sink.

Tubing bender
To bend flexible copper tubing without kinking it, slip a bending spring over it before you make the bend.

Tubing cutter
Use this to cut copper pipe or tubing. It's also good for plastic pipe. The pop-up part is a reamer to remove the burr inside the cut.

Choosing pipe

First you must determine what kind of pipe you have in your home. It's often easiest to use the same type when adding on, but you don't have to. To change type, you must purchase special adapter fittings that connect one material to another in the middle of a pipe run.

Supply lines—the pipes that carry pressurized water to your fixtures—usually are copper and plastic. However, if your home is old enough to have galvanized pipe and you need to install only a short run of pipe, it makes sense to continue with galvanized piping. In many localities, plastic supply pipe is not allowed. Keep in mind that you'll have to learn how to solder in order to use copper pipe (see pages 72–75).

To make final connections to a fixture or a faucet, install a flexible supply line. Use copper (see page 76) or plastic flexible tubing and be careful to avoid kinks.

Plastic pipe—either PVC (polyvinyl chloride) or ABS (acrylonitrile-butadiene-styrene)—is now used almost exclusively for drains. If you have old cast-iron, galvanized, or copper drainpipes, make the transition to plastic for new work. It is much easier to install and less expensive.

Before you buy any pipe, check with the local building department to make sure the material is approved for use in your locale.

CPVC

PVC

ABS

Black steel

Galvanized steel

Flexible copper

Rigid copper

Cast iron

Flexible PE

Flexible PB

PEX

GAS LINES

Gas lines are almost always made of black steel pipe. It is like galvanized steel pipe but is not zinc-coated. You install black steel pipe the same way you install galvanized pipe (see page 81). Check for leaks by turning the gas on, brushing soapy water on the joints, and looking for bubbles.

Some local building codes allow galvanized pipe for gas and some require it outdoors. Some codes do not allow it for any gas lines.

Do not use copper pipe for long gas lines. A chemical reaction causes the inside of the pipe to flake, and a buildup of flakes can clog appliances.

COMMON PIPE SIZES

These are nominal pipe sizes (pages 70–71) commonly used in residential plumbing in North America:
- The main water supply line that enters a house is ¾ or 1 inch.
- Hot and cold water supply lines inside the house are ½-inch pipe, sometimes ¾-inch pipe.

- Gas lines are most often ¾-inch and sometimes ½-inch pipe.
- Main drainpipes, called stacks, are 3 or 4 inches in diameter.
- Kitchen, tub, and shower drains are almost always 1½-inch pipes.
- Bathroom sink drains are almost always 1¼-inch pipes.

CHOOSING PIPE

Material	Type	Uses (check local codes)	Features and joining techniques
Copper	Rigid	Hot and cold supply lines; rarely for DWV (drain-waste-vent) lines	Sold in 10' and 20' lengths. The most widely used pipe for supply lines. Lightweight and durable, though a bit expensive. Once you learn the soldering technique, it goes together quickly. Type M is the thinnest and is a good choice for home projects. Types L and K are used mainly in commercial projects.
	Flexible	Hot and cold supply lines, for short final runs to fixtures	Comes in easy-to-bend 60' and 100' coils, or by the foot. Can be soldered like rigid copper but usually is connected with compression fittings.
Threaded steel	Galvanized	Supply and occasionally DWV	Because it's cumbersome to work with and tends to build up lime deposits that constrict water flow, it is not used widely anymore. Expensive equipment is required to cut and thread it, so users must buy precut pieces from suppliers. If you have a good selection of shorter pieces on hand, you can cut down on trips to the supplier.
	Black	Gas lines	Rusts readily, so it can't be used for water supply.
Plastic	ABS	DWV only	Black in color, in 10' or 20' lengths. Lightweight and easy to work with, it cuts with an ordinary saw and cements together with a special glue. Check local codes before using.
	PVC	Cold water supply and DWV	Cream color, blue-gray, or white, PVC comes in 10' or 20' lengths. This has the same properties as ABS, except that you must apply primer before cementing it. Do not mix PVC with ABS or interchange their cements.
	CPVC	Hot and cold supply lines	White, gray, or cream color, CPVC is available in 10' lengths. Has the same properties as ABS and PVC.
	Flexible PB (polybutylene)	Hot and cold supply lines, usually for short runs	White or cream color, flexible PB is sold in 25' or 100' coils or by the foot. Expensive and not widely used, it is joined with special fittings.
	Flexible PE (polyethylene)	Supply lines	Black color, sold in 25' or 100' coils or by the foot. Same properties as PB. Used for sprinkler systems.
	PEX	Hot and cold supply lines	Resembles red hose, sold in 25' or 100' coils or by the foot. Expensive, but easy to install; crimp fittings.
Cast iron	Hub-and-spigot	DWV	Extremely heavy and difficult to work with, so don't try to install new pipes of this material. Hub-and-spigot is joined with oakum and molten lead.
	No-hub	DWV	Joins with gaskets and clamps but still is hard to work with. Make the transition to plastic instead.

Choosing fittings

COPPER SUPPLY

The parts bins at plumbing suppliers contain hundreds of fittings that allow you to connect and interconnect various pipe materials. To get the best pipe for your needs, familiarize yourself with the terms on this page.

Supply fittings connect the pipes that bring water to fixtures and faucets. When changing direction in a supply run, use an elbow (ell). The most common ones make 90- or 45-degree turns and have female threads on each end. A street ell has male and female connections to allow for insertion into another fitting. A reducing ell joins one size pipe to another. Use a drop ell to anchor the pipes to framing where they will protrude into a room.

Use tees wherever two runs intersect. A reducing tee lets you join pipes of different diameters; for example, if you want to add a 1/2-inch branch to a 3/4-inch main supply.

A coupling connects pipes end to end. Reducing couplings let you step down from one pipe diameter to a smaller one. Slip couplings function the same way unions do, joining sections of copper or plastic line. Use a cap to seal off a line.

A plastic-to-copper transition fitting is one of many transition fittings that connect one pipe material to another. (Do not make the transition from steel to copper without a special dielectric fitting, or the joint will corrode.)

In any run of threaded pipe, you'll need a union somewhere. This fitting

GALVANIZED SUPPLY

compensates for the frustrating fact that you can't simultaneously turn a pipe into fittings at either end.

Nipples—pipes less than 12 inches long—are available in standard sizes because short pieces are difficult to cut and thread.

Examine drainage fittings and you'll see how they're designed to keep wastewater flowing downhill. Sometimes called sanitary fittings, they have gentle curves rather than sharp angles, so waste won't get hung up.

Choose 1/4 bends to make 90-degree turns and 1/8 bends for 45 degrees. Also available are 1/5 bends for 72-degree turns and 1/6 bends for 60 degrees. All types of bends also come in more gradual curves, known as long-turn bends, which make for a smoother flow.

Sanitary branches, such as the tee and cross, come in a variety of configurations that suit situations where two or more lines converge. These can be tricky to order, so make a sketch of your proposed drain lines, identifying all pipe sizes, and take it to your supplier when you order.

Toilet hookups require a closet bend, which connects to the main drain, and a closet flange, which fits onto the bend. The flange is anchored to the floor and anchors the toilet bowl. To connect a sink trap to the drainpipe, use a trap adapter. To make the transition from cast-iron drain to plastic drain, use a no-hub adapter.

PLASTIC SUPPLY

PLASTIC DRAIN

ORDERING OR FINDING FITTINGS

When ordering materials, organize your description of a fitting in this way: first the size, then the material, and finally the type of fitting. You might, for example, ask or look for a 1/2-inch galvanized 90-degree ell. With reducing fittings, the larger size comes first, then the smaller.

PEX

90-degree elbow | 45-degree elbow | Tee | Coupling | Reducing coupling | Drop ell | Cap

Elbow | Reducing tee | Nipple | Union | Cap | Copper-to-steel transition

90-degree ell | Tee | Coupling | Reducing coupling | ⅛ (45-degree) bend | Trap adapter for transition from galvanized steel to plastic | Drop ell plastic-to-copper transition | Plastic-to-copper transition fitting

¼ (90-degree) long-turn bend

Sanitary cross

Closet bend

Drain trap

Sanitary tee

Closet flange

Trap adapter

Plastic-to-cast-iron no-hub fitting

Drop-ear elbow | Crimp elbow | Crimp tee | Male adapter | Female adapter | Crimp ring | Crimp plug | Swivel connector | Crimp valve

Measuring pipes and fittings

I t takes practice and experience to be able to determine all the pipes and fittings you will need before starting a job, so novice plumbers often spend more time running back and forth to their supplier than they do on the actual work. The first step in becoming an efficient plumber is to learn to correctly identify the pipes and fittings for a job.

Plumbing dimensions aren't necessarily what they appear to be. A plastic pipe with a $7/8$-inch outside diameter, for instance, is actually called a $1/2$-inch pipe because it has a $1/2$-inch inside diameter (ID). Pipes usually are sized according to their ID (see chart below). This dimension is also called the nominal size, the size you ask for at a plumbing supplier.

To find a pipe's size, measure the inside ...

If you have a pipe with an exposed end, simply measure the pipe's inside diameter and round off to the nearest $1/8$ inch. Some manufacturers indicate the nominal pipe size on the fittings.

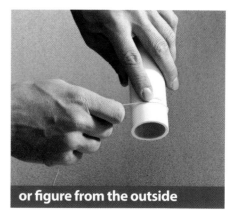

or figure from the outside

You also can determine pipe size by measuring its outside circumference. Wrap a string around the pipe, straighten it out, and measure it. Use the chart below to find the nominal size you'll need to order.

MEASUREMENTS: PIPE DIMENSIONS

Material	Inside diameter (ID) nominal size	Approximate outside diameter (OD)	Approximate circumference	Approximate socket depth
Copper	$1/4$"	$3/8$"	$1 1/8$"	$5/16$"
	$3/8$"	$1/2$"	$1 1/2$"	$3/8$"
	$1/2$"	$5/8$"	2"	$1/2$"
	$3/4$"	$7/8$"	$2 3/4$"	$3/4$"
	1"	$1 1/8$"	$3 1/2$"	$15/16$"
	$1 1/4$"	$1 3/8$"	$4 5/16$"	1"
	$1 1/2$"	$1 5/8$"	$5 1/8$"	$1 1/8$"
Threaded steel	$3/8$"	$5/8$"	2"	$3/8$"
	$1/2$"	$3/4$"	$2 3/8$"	$1/2$"
	$3/4$"	1"	$3 1/8$"	$9/16$"
	1"	$1 1/4$"	4"	$11/16$"
	$1 1/4$"	$1 1/2$"	$4 3/4$"	$11/16$"
	$1 1/2$"	$1 3/4$"	$5 1/2$"	$11/16$"
	2"	$2 1/4$"	7"	$3/4$"
Plastic	$1/2$"	$7/8$"	$2 3/4$"	$1/2$"
	$3/4$"	$1 1/8$"	$3 1/2$"	$5/8$"
	1"	$1 3/8$"	$4 5/16$"	$3/4$"
	$1 1/4$"	$1 5/8$"	$5 1/8$"	$11/16$"
	$1 1/2$"	$1 7/8$"	6"	$11/16$"
	2"	$2 3/8$"	$7 1/2$"	$3/4$"
	3"	$3 3/8$"	$10 1/2$"	$1 1/2$"
	4"	$4 3/8$"	$13 3/4$"	$1 3/4$"
Cast iron	2"	$2 1/4$"	7"	$2 1/2$"
	3"	$3 1/4$"	$10 1/8$"	$2 3/4$"
	4"	$4 1/4$"	$13 3/8$"	3"

If you are unsure about getting the right material, specify the ID for most pipes. In the case of tubing—flexible copper lines, for example—the nominal size is the outside diameter (OD).

If you can measure the inside dimension, your job is easier. However, often you won't have a way of measuring the inside of the pipe. Holding a ruler against a pipe will give you only a rough idea of the outside diameter. Instead, use a string or a set of calipers for a more exact measurement. Once you find the outside dimension, use the chart, opposite, to find the nominal size. It is often easier to take a short piece of the pipe you need to the store with you.

Fittings can be just as confusing. Their inside diameters must be large enough to fit over the pipe's outside diameter. A ½-inch plastic elbow, for example, has an outside diameter of about 1¼ inches.

As a rule of thumb, copper pipe's OD is ⅛ inch greater than its ID, the nominal size. For plastic pipe, measure the OD and subtract ⅜ inch. For threaded and cast-iron pipe, subtract ¼ inch. Again, you can take a short piece of pipe to the store to make sure you get the right fittings.

Another mathematical pitfall for a novice plumber is measuring the length of a pipe that runs from one fitting to the next. Pipes must fully extend into fixture and fitting sockets (see illustrations, right), or the joint could leak. Socket depths vary from one pipe size and material to another, so you must account for the depth of each fitting's socket in the total length of pipe needed between fittings.

The only times you don't have to take socket depth into account are when you are using no-hub cast-iron pipes (see page 125) or slip couplings with copper or plastic pipe.

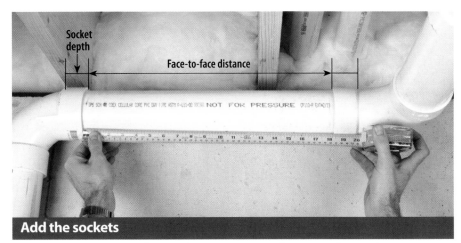

Socket depth

Face-to-face distance

NOT FOR PRESSURE

Add the sockets

To determine the length of a pipe, first measure from face to face, as shown above. Then check the chart on the opposite page for the socket depth of the

material you're working with. Because pipes have fittings on both ends, multiply by 2 and add the face-to-face length.

FULLY JOINED PIPE

Socket depth

Copper

ID equals OD minus ⅛"

Socket depth

Plastic

ID equals OD minus ⅜"

Socket depth

Threaded

ID equals OD minus ¼"

MEASURE COPPER OR PLASTIC IN PLACE

When working with copper or plastic—materials you can cut on the job—often the most accurate way of measuring is to insert the pipe into one fitting and mark the other end, rather than using a tape measure.

GET A BUNCH OF CAPS

Don't leave the household high and dry while you drive back and forth to the plumbing supplier. When buying fittings, invest in a handful of caps in different sizes. That way, if you've misread a dimension—as even experienced plumbers do occasionally—you can easily cap off the line and turn the water on again.

Working with rigid copper pipe

TIME: With practice, 1 hour to connect five joints
SKILLS: Soldering is a specialized skill that takes time to learn
TOOLS: Tubing cutter or hacksaw, emery cloth, wire brush, flux brush, solder, rags, propane torch, groove-joint pliers

Soldering rigid copper plumbing takes some time to learn, but once you get the knack, soldering is quicker than screwing together threaded pipe.

Soldering is often called "sweating." Capillary action draws molten solder into the joint to make a watertight bond that's as strong as the pipe itself.

DRY THE PIPES

Pipes must be dry before soldering. If possible, tilt the pipes to allow water to flow out. Heat the pipe to evaporate remaining moisture; open faucets on the line to let steam escape.

A piece of white bread (not the crust) stuffed in upstream of the connection will absorb the water and dissolve when the water is turned on. You can also buy capsules that plug the line while you work. When the work is finished, heat from a torch melts the capsule away.

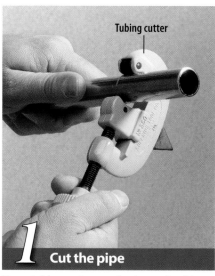

1 Cut the pipe

Use a tubing cutter or a hacksaw. A tubing cutter makes cleaner cuts. Clamp the cutter onto the tubing, rotate a few revolutions, tighten, and rotate some more. Make hacksaw cuts in a miter box. Don't nick the metal—this could cause the connection to leak.

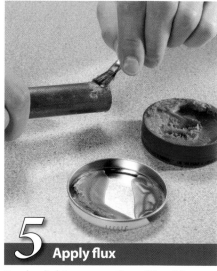

2 Remove the burrs

Remove burrs on the inside of the pipe by inserting the reaming blade of the tubing cutter and twisting. If you don't have a tubing cutter, use a metal file.

3 Dry-fit the pieces

Dry-fit a number of pipe pieces and fittings to make sure they are the right length. If you have difficulty pushing pieces together because the pipe was squeezed out of shape during cutting, cut a new piece. Most pros lay out an entire run of copper, cutting and dry-fitting all of its components. Once you are satisfied, take the pipes apart and set them on a clean surface.

4 Polish the pipe and fitting

Clean the outside of the pipe with emery cloth and the inside of the fitting with a wire brush. The surface must be clean and shiny for best results when soldering.

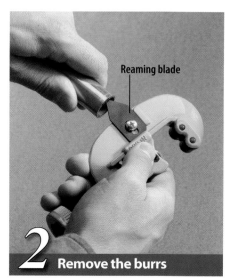

5 Apply flux

Brush a light, even coating of flux (also called soldering paste) onto both surfaces. Flux retards oxidation when the copper is heated. As solder flows into the joint, the flux burns away. Use a resin- (not acid-) type flux for plumbing work. Assemble the joint components.

6 Form the solder

To make the solder easy to handle and to keep your fingers away from the flame, unwind about 10 inches of solder, straighten it, and bend a 60-degree angle about 2 inches from the end. Light the torch. Adjust the flame until the inner (blue) cone is about 2 inches long.

7 Protect flammable surfaces

If you're working near framing, paper-sheathed insulation, or other flammable materials, shield them from the propane torch flame with an old cookie sheet or a piece of sheet metal.

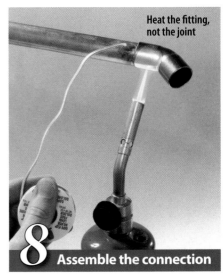

Heat the fitting, not the joint

8 Assemble the connection

Heat the middle of the fitting—not the joint—with the inner cone of the flame. Touch the solder to the joint. If it is hot enough, capillary action will pull solder into the joint. Remove the flame when solder drips from the pipe.

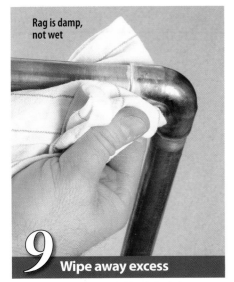

Rag is damp, not wet

9 Wipe away excess

For a neat, professional look, lightly wipe around the joint with a damp rag. Take care not to burn your fingers.

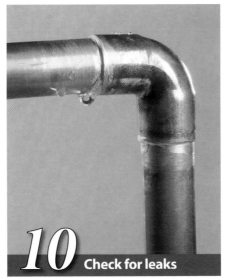

10 Check for leaks

Turn on the water to test the system. If you have a leak, there is no easy solution—you can't fix a leak while water is present. Shut off the water, drain the line, disassemble the joint (see page 74), and discard the old fitting. Dry the inside of the pipes. Polish the pipe end and the inside of the new fitting, apply flux, reassemble, and solder.

11 Install pipe hangers

Copper supply lines need support at least every 6 feet. The plastic type of hanger shown is easy to install, helps quiet noisy pipes, and is slightly flexible so it doesn't damage the pipes.

Working with rigid copper pipe *(continued)*

Installing a brass valve

Brass valve

1 Remove heat-sensitive parts

A valve stem has rubber or plastic parts that will melt during soldering. Remove the stem with a wrench. Polish the pipe end and the inside of the fitting as you would a copper joint.

2 Solder the joint

Fit the pieces together. If the valve has an arrow, be sure it points in the direction of water flow. Heat the body of the valve, moving the flame back and forth to heat both sides evenly. Brass requires more heating than copper. Apply solder as you would with a copper fitting.

Taking apart soldering joints

1 Heat the fittings

Shut off the water and drain the line. Light a propane torch, set it so the inner (blue) cone of the flame is about 2 inches long, and heat the fitting. Point the flame at both sides of the fitting, not directly at the soldered joint.

2 Pull the pieces apart

Once the fitting is heated, you have only a few seconds to take the joint apart. Prepare a safe place to set the torch and have two pairs of pliers within easy reach. Work carefully—the pipes are very hot. While the pipe is hot, grasp the fitting and pipe with pliers and pull the joint apart.

3 Polish the pipe ends

To remove old solder, heat the pipe end with the torch and quickly wipe with a dry rag. Do this carefully—the pipe is very hot. Allow the pipe to cool and polish the end with emery cloth. Never reuse old copper fittings—only a new fitting can create a watertight seal.

Using a propane torch

Use the torch safely

A propane torch produces carbon monoxide, which is odorless, colorless, and toxic in a confined space. Open a window and position a small fan to remove fumes from the work area.

Read the instructions provided by the manufacturer of the propane torch. Pay special attention to the cylinder seals and torch nozzles. If you see any damage, return the torch to the store and exchange it for a new one.

To light the torch, open the valve and strike a spark in front of the torch tip with a spark lighter or activate the built-in lighter. Adjust the valve so the blue flame is 1 to 2 inches long.

Always close the torch valve when you are finished with it. Hand-tighten the valve but be careful not to overtighten it.

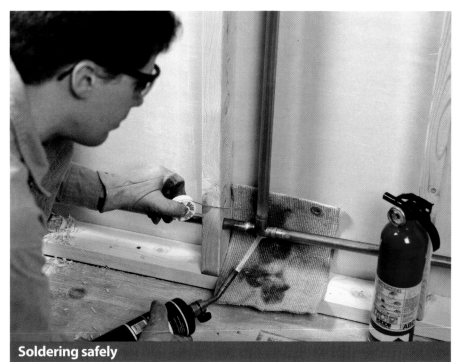

Soldering safely

Running a new copper supply line requires negotiating turns and working in tight places. You may find yourself having to solder fittings inside confining access panels and between floor joists. Inspect each area. A propane torch produces a flame. Look for potential fire hazards. Isolate them or place a protective barrier between the joint to be soldered and the flammable object. You can purchase a flameproof barrier at your local home center or hardware store. The barriers are constructed of a flame-retardant material. Some manufacturers put grommets in the corners to allow you to hang or nail them in place, thus freeing your hands. An old cookie sheet also works as an excellent barrier. As an added safety measure, always keep a fire extinguisher handy while working.

SOLDERING SAFETY TIPS

Soldering hazards include fumes and possible burns—the solder and propane torch are hot enough to instantly burn flesh. Use the following rules for safe soldering.

- Wear eye protection, either a face shield or safety glasses. Eyes may become irritated when exposed to the smoke. Avoid wearing contact lenses as the fumes can get under the lenses and cause severe irritation.
- Avoid breathing smoke/fumes produced during soldering. Use a small fan to remove the fumes. Inhaling flux fumes during soldering may cause irritation and damage of mucous membranes and the respiratory system.
- When ventilating the room is not sufficient or when working in close quarters, wear an approved respirator.
- Cover legs and arms to avoid burns from splashed hot solder.
- Wash your hands thoroughly after handling solder. Use only lead-free solder.

Working with flexible copper tubing

- **TIME:** About 15 minutes to bend and cut tubing for a short run
- **SKILLS:** Handling and cutting copper tubing
- **TOOLS:** Tubing cutter, coil-spring tubing bender

Flexible copper tubing is pliable enough to make all but the sharpest turns. When you use it, you don't have to install a fitting every time you make a turn as you would with rigid pipe. In almost every case, you will connect flexible tubing to compression and flare fittings (see pages 77–79) instead of soldering it.

Do not use copper tubing for a gas line. Natural gas will cause the inside of the copper tube to flake, which can damage appliances.

POLISH THE END

To complete your work with flexible copper tubing, rub the end of the tubing lightly with emery cloth to remove dirt and grease. With compression or flare fittings, you don't need to polish as much as you do for a soldered joint. To join tubing, solder the pieces together (see pages 72–75), or use compression fittings (see pages 77–78) or flare fittings (see page 79).

1 Uncoil the tubing

Handle flexible copper tubing gently because it is soft. As you uncoil tubing, straighten it out every few inches as you go. If the tubing comes in a box, grip the box and carefully pull the tubing out.

2 Cut the tubing

Cut copper tubing with a tubing cutter. To remove burrs on the inside of the cut end, insert the reaming blade of the tubing cutter into the end and twist it or use a metal file.

Kinked tubing

Coil-spring tubing bender

Bend the tubing

Bend the flexible tubing in gradual sweeping arcs. If you don't, it will surprise you by suddenly kinking and you'll have to throw the piece away. Kinks seriously impede water flow and are almost impossible to reshape.

If you must make a make a fairly tight bend, use a coil-spring tubing bender as shown. Slide the tool over the tubing to the point where you need the tight turn and bend the tubing. Then slide the bender off the tubing.

Compression fittings

■ **TIME:** About 15 minutes to make a simple connection
■ **SKILLS:** No special skills needed
■ **TOOLS:** Two adjustable wrenches, pipe joint compound

Compression fittings are ideal in places where you may need to take the joint apart someday or where it is difficult to solder. One common location is on supply lines for a sink, which have compression fittings at both the stop valve and the faucet inlet. Flexible supply tubes make this connection even easier (see page 29).

Compression fittings usually are used with flexible copper tubing, but you can also use type-M rigid copper (see pages 66–67). These fittings are not as strong as soldered joints, so they should not be hidden inside walls.

Use compression fittings to connect plastic supply tubing for refrigerator icemakers. The difference between a compression fitting designed for copper and one designed for plastic tubing is that the copper fitting will have a metal compression ring, while the plastic fitting will have a plastic compression ring. Using the wrong fitting on the wrong material will create leaks, so don't do it. Other than the one difference between the two fittings, installation is the same for both.

Never overtighten a fitting, especially when using plastic tubing. Once you encounter resistance when tightening, don't be tempted to give it an additional half-turn. Test the integrity of the connection first. Slightly open the water supply valve. If it leaks, turn the water off and tighten the compression nut a quarter-turn. Retest the line. If it continues to leak, tighten a quarter-turn and test each time until the leak stops.

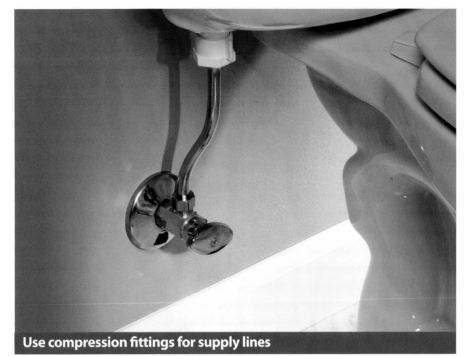

Use compression fittings for supply lines

Compression fittings are commonly used on fixtures where you may need to disconnect them in the future.

Common locations are on supply lines for sinks and toilets.

1 To make a compression joint, position the parts

Bend the tubing into position and slip on the nut and the ferrule. The ferrule will not go on if the tubing end isn't perfectly round. You may have to sand the tubing with emery cloth to get the ferrule to slide on. Smear pipe joint compound on the ferrule and the male threads of the fitting.

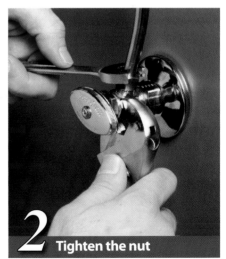

2 Tighten the nut

Seat the tubing in the fitting and tighten the compression nut with a wrench, forcing the ferrule into the tubing to secure and seal the connection. If the joint leaks when the water is turned on, tighten the nut a quarter-turn at a time until the leak stops. Be careful—too much pressure can crush the tubing or crack the nut.

Compression fittings *(continued)*

Installing a compression union

1 Align the connecting lines

Bend the tubing sections into position (see page 76). Slip a nut and a ferrule onto each piece of tubing.

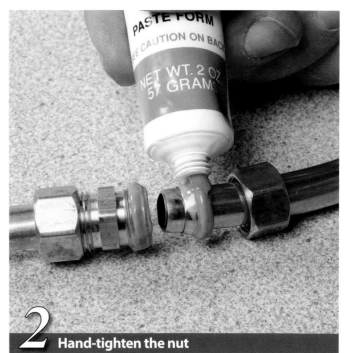

2 Hand-tighten the nut

Apply pipe joint compound on the ferrules and on the male threads of the union. Slide the pieces together, seat the tubing in the fitting, and hand-tighten the nut on one side. Seat the tubing and hand-tighten the nut on the other side.

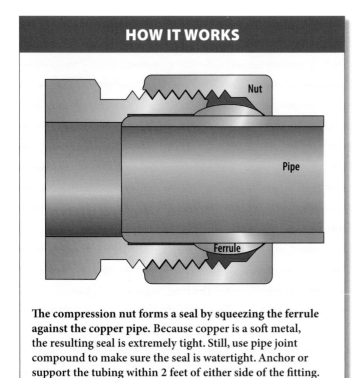

HOW IT WORKS

Nut

Pipe

Ferrule

The compression nut forms a seal by squeezing the ferrule against the copper pipe. Because copper is a soft metal, the resulting seal is extremely tight. Still, use pipe joint compound to make sure the seal is watertight. Anchor or support the tubing within 2 feet of either side of the fitting.

3 Tighten each side

Grip the union with one wrench and use another wrench to tighten each side. Once snug, tighten a half-turn more. Turn on the water to check for leaks. If it leaks, gently tighten more.

Flare fittings

■ **TIME:** About 30 minutes to join two pieces together in a union
■ **SKILLS:** Using a flaring tool
■ **TOOLS:** Flaring tool, adjustable wrenches

Flare fittings, like compression fittings, are useful in places where it's difficult to solder a joint. Don't hide flare fittings inside a wall. You can use flare fittings only with flexible copper tubing, not on rigid pipe. Unlike compression fittings, this type of fitting requires a flaring tool. The two-piece tool reshapes the end of the copper tubing, "flaring" it to fit into a special flare fitting. Sometimes the tubing splits while being flared, so, if possible, make the flared connection first, then cut the tubing to length.

1 Flare the tubing ends

Slip the flare nut on before you flare the end of the tubing. Choose the hole in the flaring block that matches the outside diameter of the tubing. Clamp the tool onto the tubing. Align the compression cone on the tubing's end and tighten the screw. As you turn the handle, the cone flares the tubing's end. Inspect your work carefully after removing the tubing from the block. If the end has split, cut off the flared portion and repeat the process.

2 Assemble the pieces

Seat the flare union against one of the flared ends of the tubing, slide the nut down, and hand-tighten. Do the same on the other side. Pipe joint compound is not necessary.

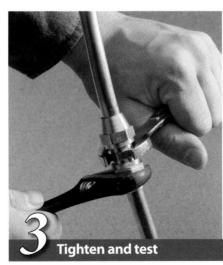

3 Tighten and test

Place one wrench on the union and one on a nut. Don't overtighten a flared joint. Once snug, give each nut a half-turn. Turn the water on and test. If the joint leaks, tighten it carefully until the leak stops. If the leak persists, dismantle the joint and examine it to see if the tubing was cut squarely. Make sure that the nut was not cross-threaded on the fitting. Anchor or support the tubing within 2 feet of either side of the flare fitting.

Removing old threaded pipe

- **TIME:** About 1 hour to take apart four or five sections of pipe with fittings
- **SKILLS:** Use of a pipe wrench and sometimes brute strength
- **TOOLS:** Two pipe wrenches, hacksaw, maybe a propane torch

Once you have worked with threaded pipe, you'll understand why it is so rarely used now for new water pipes. Cutting, threading, and assembling steel pipe requires muscle and specialized equipment. When you're trying to take old pipe apart, you'll swear it is welded together.

If your home was built before World War II, its supply pipes are likely made of threaded steel. This doesn't mean you have to use the same pipe for improvements or repairs. Special fittings enable you to break into a line and add copper or plastic (see pages 68–69).

Black threaded pipe, which lacks the zinc coating of galvanized pipe, is intended for gas lines only and is still commonly used. Don't use black pipe for water lines; it rusts quickly. Some codes don't allow the use of galvanized pipe for gas lines.

SWITCHING MATERIALS

If your water pressure is adequate and you find little rust trapped in your aerators, there is no need to replace threaded steel pipe with copper or plastic. But if water pressure is low, aerators fill up with rust, and leaks develop, it is a good idea to change. Replace long, horizontal lines first. Avoid cutting holes into walls unless it is absolutely necessary. PEX pipe (page 86) is easiest to run in walls.

Union

End

1 Start at a union

Shut off water and drain the pipes. Examine the way your pipes and fittings thread together and you'll see that you can't begin unscrewing them just anywhere. Somewhere in every pipe run is a union that allows you to unlock and dismantle the piping. To crack open a union, determine which of the ends the large union nut is threaded onto. With one wrench on the union nut and one on the union end, turn the union nut counterclockwise. Once it's unthreaded, you have the break you need and can start unscrewing pipes from fittings. When unscrewing pipe, use the second wrench to keep the fitting from turning.

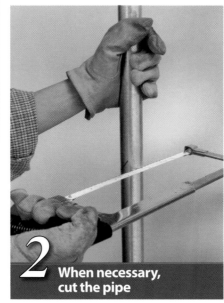

2 When necessary, cut the pipe

Without a union, you'll have to cut a pipe with a hacksaw or a reciprocating saw fitted with a metal-cutting blade. When you reassemble the run, you can install a union using prethreaded nipples on either side of the union.

3 If the pipe won't budge

Stubborn joints may respond to penetrating oil, or you can try heating the fitting with a propane torch. Try a larger pipe wrench or slip a piece of 1¼-inch or 1½-inch pipe onto the handle of your wrench to increase its leverage.

Installing threaded pipe

- **TIME:** In 1 hour you can assemble about four pipe lengths with fittings
- **SKILLS:** Pipe measuring, use of pipe wrench
- **TOOLS:** Tape measure, two pipe wrenches

If you work with threaded pipe, you'll face the difficulty of ending each run at the right place. Because the ends of the pipe are threaded, you can't simply cut a piece to fit, as you can with copper or plastic. (Many hardware stores and home centers will cut and thread pipe for you, however.) Purchase long pieces that make up most of the runs and have on hand plenty of couplings and a selection of nipples (short lengths of pipe that are threaded on each end) to give you options to end the run in the right spot.

BOOSTING PRESSURE

In an old house, galvanized pipes that are clogged with rust result in poor water pressure. If the problem is limited to one fixture, replace a few of the pipes that lead up to it. If the problem runs throughout the house, call in a professional.

There are companies that specialize in unclogging galvanized pipe. They use a process that causes rust and corrosion to fall away from the inside of the pipe. The process can take months to complete, will clog faucets, and may reveal leaks as the gunk is removed. In the end, however, water will flow through the pipes as if they were new.

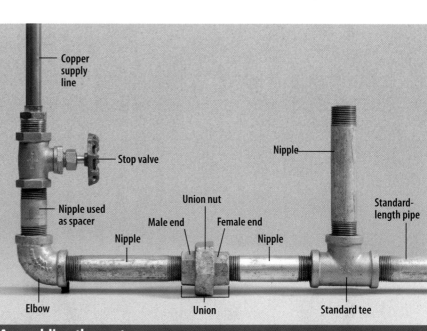

Copper supply line

Stop valve

Nipple used as spacer

Nipple

Male end

Union nut

Female end

Nipple

Nipple

Standard-length pipe

Elbow

Union

Standard tee

Assembling the parts

This typical installation combines standard-length pipes with joints and nipples to end up exactly at the right location. (For background on measuring pipe accurately, see pages 70–71.) Many plumbing suppliers offer ready-cut steel pipe in standard lengths—12 inches, 48 inches, and so on—for less cost (and delay) than custom-cut pieces. Try to use standard-size pieces; if you make a mistake in measuring a custom-cut pipe, it is probably not returnable.

Pipe joint compound

Joint tape

Joining the pieces

Before you thread a pipe and fitting together, seal the pipe threads using pipe joint compound or joint tape. Assemble the pipes and fittings one at a time, tightening each as you go. If your assembly requires a union, work from each end toward the union. The union is installed last. Support runs of threaded pipe at least every 6 feet.

Working with rigid plastic pipe

- **TIME:** With practice, you can cut and install about five fittings and five pieces of pipe in 1 hour
- **SKILLS:** Measuring, cutting, and assembling components
- **TOOLS:** Plastic pipe saw or hacksaw, miter box, tape measure, utility knife, marker, emery cloth, plastic tubing cutter for supply lines

Plastic plumbing is popular with do-it-yourselfers because it is inexpensive and easy to work with. Plastic pipe cuts with an ordinary hacksaw and goes together without special tools or techniques. You simply clean the burrs from the cut, prime, and glue the parts together.

Installing plastic pipe requires attention to detail, planning ahead, and doing things in the right order. If you make a mistake, the cemented parts can't be disassembled. You'll have to cut out the faulty section, throw it away, and start again.

You'll find various types of plastic, so check local codes to make sure you're using the right type for your purpose. In most localities, either ABS or PVC is accepted (sometimes even required) for drain lines. Many localities do not accept plastic pipe for supply lines; others specify CPVC (see pages 66–67). Do not mix ABS with PVC. Each expands at a different rate and requires a different cement. Plastic pipe is not as stiff as metal; be sure to support horizontal runs every 4 to 5 feet.

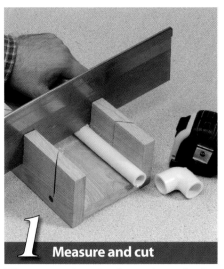

1 Measure and cut

When measuring pipe for cutting, take the socket depth of the fitting into account (see pages 70–71). Cut with any fine-tooth saw, using a miter box. Avoid crooked cuts because they reduce the bonding area at the deepest part of the fitting's socket—the most critical part of the joint.

2 Remove burrs from the cut end

After you've made the cut, use a deburring tool (shown), knife, or file to remove any burrs from the inside and outside of the cut end. Burrs can scrape away cement as the pipe is pushed into the fitting, weakening the bond.

3 Test the fitting

Dry-fit the connection. You should be able to push it in at least one-third of the way. If the pipe bottoms out and feels loose, try another fitting. Unlike copper components, plastic pipes are made with tapered walls on the inside of the socket so that the pipe makes contact well before it reaches the socket shoulder.

4 Mark for alignment

When gluing the pieces together, you will have less than a minute to correctly position the pipe and fitting before the glue sets. Draw an alignment mark across the pipe and fitting of each joint. When you fit the pieces together, the mark will indicate exactly how to position the pipe and fitting.

5 Clean and prime

Wipe the inside of the fitting and the outside of the pipe end with a clean cloth. If you are working with PVC or CPVC (but not ABS), coat the outside of the pipe end with a special primer. Many inspectors require purple-colored primer so they can easily see that joints have been primed.

6 Apply cement to pipe

Use the cement designed for the material you're working with. Immediately after you've primed, swab a smooth coating of cement onto the pipe end.

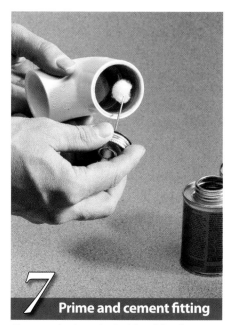

7 Prime and cement fitting

Clean and prime the inside of the fitting socket. Apply cement liberally but don't let it puddle inside the fitting. Reapply a coating of cement to the pipe end.

8 Twist and hold

Push the two pieces together, ensuring the pipe seats fully into the socket. Twist a quarter-turn as you push to help spread the cement evenly. Complete the twist until your alignment marks come together. Hold the pipe and fitting together for about 20 seconds while they fuse into a single piece. Wipe away excess cement.

Cut off any incorrect joints

If you misalign a connection, saw it off squarely. Install a new fitting with a spacer and slip coupling, as shown. Cemented joints are strong enough to handle after 15 minutes, but don't run water in the line for about two hours.

DRY-FIT THREE OR FOUR PIECES AHEAD

Whenever possible, cut and dry-fit three or four pieces before priming and gluing. That way, you can get things lined up ahead of time and avoid going back and forth between cans of primer and cement.

However, don't dry-fit more than four pieces and don't dry-fit an entire section that must come out to an exact length. Plastic is not like copper pipe, which will solder together exactly the way it was dry-fitted. Once the cement is applied, plastic pipes may slide farther in than they did during the dry run, throwing off measurements as much as 1/4 inch per fitting.

Working with ABS pipe

■ **TIME:** Varies depending on the project

■ **SKILLS:** Connecting fittings, using a miter box or tubing cutter

■ **TOOLS:** Tape measure, backsaw and miter box, hacksaw, or pipe cutter, deburring tool or emery cloth, marker, cloth

Many homes built in the 1960s and 1970s have ABS (acrylonitrile-butadiene-styrene) drainpipes. ABS is now banned for use in many locales, because it sometimes becomes brittle or shrinks, causing joints to leak. PVC is generally considered superior to ABS and is required by many local codes.

If your home has ABS pipe, you probably do not have to replace it. However, codes may require that you use PVC pipe for new installations. If so, be sure to use an approved ABS/PVC transition fitting when joining the new to the old. In many locales, it is difficult if not impossible to buy new ABS pipe.

If codes allow the use of ABS, cut and install it as shown.

1 Use ABS cleaner and cement

Be sure to use products made for joining ABS pipe. ABS joints are made with cleaner, rather than primer, and ABS cement. Apply cleaner, such as the all-purpose product shown, to the pipe before applying the cement.

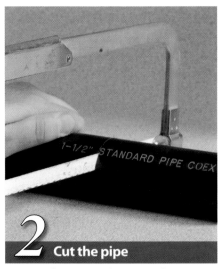

2 Cut the pipe

Measure for cutting the pipe, taking into account the distance the pipe will travel inside the fittings. Cut ABS pipe using a hacksaw, a plastic pipe saw, or a power mitersaw. Take care to make square cuts; an angled cut makes for a weak joint.

3 Clean and glue

Remove all burrs from the inside and outside of the pipe using a deburring tool, sandpaper, or a knife. Assemble a dry run of pipes and fittings, to make sure they all fit (page 83). Draw alignment marks wherever a fitting needs to face in a certain direction.

Disassemble the dry run, placing the parts in order for reassembly. Wipe the insides of the fittings and the outsides of the pipes clean and apply ABS cleaner.

Cement the joints one at a time. To make a connection, use the dauber to apply cement to the pipe end and to the inside of the fitting. Within a few seconds, insert the pipe into the fitting, twisting slightly as you push. Hold the fitting still for 20 seconds or so, then wipe away any excess cement. After all the pieces have been connected, wait two hours before running water through them.

Working with CPVC

- **TIME:** Varies depending on the project
- **SKILLS:** Connecting fittings, using a miter box or tubing cutter
- **TOOLS:** Tape measure, saw and miter box or pipe cutter, deburring tool or emery cloth, marker, cloth

Chlorinated polyvinyl chloride (CPVC) pipe, tubing, and fittings can be used in both hot- and cold-water supply systems. CPVC is often the material of choice for outdoor installations. However, many local codes do not permit its use for interior installations; you may need to install copper instead. Some codes require special "proof testing" of CPVC assemblies; contact your local building inspector to find out if this is required and how to do it.

WORKING WITH CPVC CHECKLIST

- Make sure all cements and primers are made for use with CPVC pipe.
- Keep all pipe and fittings in original packaging until needed.
- Use tools designed for use with plastic pipe and fittings.
- Cut all pipe ends square.
- Deburr and bevel the pipe ends.
- Rotate the pipe at least a quarter-turn when bottoming the pipe into the fitting socket.
- Avoid puddling cement in fittings and pipe.
- Follow the cement manufacturer's recommended cure times before pressure testing.
- Support the pipe with plastic pipe straps that fully encircle the pipe.
- When running pipe through wood studs, drill holes 1/4 inch larger than the outside diameter of the tube.
- Use protective pipe isolators when running through metal studs.

1 Use the right tools and materials

Buy primer and cement made specifically for joining CPVC pipe instead of all-purpose products. Follow local codes. Most inspectors require highly visible purple primer so they can quickly see that you have primed the joints. Choose cans that have daubers about half the diameter of the fittings. Larger daubers make a mess and smaller daubers do not apply enough cement or primer. To quickly cut pipe, buy a pipe cutter made for use with your size pipe.

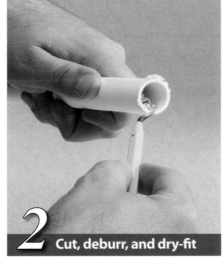

2 Cut, deburr, and dry-fit

Measure for pipe cuts, taking into account the distance the pipe goes into the fittings. Draw cut lines using a felt-tipped marker. Cut the pipe using a pipe cutter, hacksaw, pipe saw, or power mitersaw. Make the cuts square; an angled cut will weaken the joint. Use a pipe deburring tool, a knife, or a piece of sandpaper to remove the burrs. Assemble several pipes and fittings in a dry run. Once you are sure they all fit correctly, make alignment marks wherever a fitting needs to face a certain direction.

3 Cement a joint

Disassemble the dry run and keep the parts in order. Wipe the pipes and fittings clean with a dry cloth. Apply primer to the insides of the fittings and to the outsides of the pipe ends.

Cement the joints one at a time. Apply cement with a dauber, first to the inside of the fitting and then to the pipe end. Immediately insert the pipe into the fitting, twisting slightly as you push. Hold the fitting still for 20 seconds or so, then wipe away excess cement. Wait two hours before running water in the pipe.

Working with PEX pipe

TIME: About 5 minutes to cut tubing and make a crimp connection

SKILLS: Measuring and cutting tubing, crimping

TOOLS: Plastic tubing cutter, PEX crimping tool

A relatively recent advance in plumbing technology, PEX pipe makes supply-line installation simpler and quicker than any other method. PEX, cross-linked polyethylene tubing, is flexible, cuts easily, and can be joined with permanent crimped connections or compression fittings.

PEX is approved by an increasing number of building codes for hot and cold water. It is ideal for replacing steel pipe in older homes and for remodeling because it can be snaked through walls much like electrical cable. Hole alignment need not be perfect.

Although the cost of PEX materials is often higher than other piping, the savings in labor time can make the installation competitive.

A PEX manifold fitting allows easy installation of several branches—cold water lines for a sink, toilet, tub, and shower—that would require complex cutting and measuring if done with rigid pipe.

In most cases, you should run the tubing first, cut it to length, then install fittings and make connections.

COMPRESSION FITTINGS

Most building codes allow plastic compression fittings for PEX only where the joint will be accessible. For other connections, make joints with a PEX crimping tool (page 65) and crimp fittings (page 69) for a permanent installation.

CONNECTING UP

To join PEX to an existing threaded pipe, crimp on a pipe-thread adapter and join the PEX and pipe with a union. Brass adapters are available that you can sweat onto copper pipe to provide a crimp fitting. Or install a manifold fitting as shown at right to connect several PEX lines to an existing pipe.

1 Install a crimp fitting

Cut the tubing to length with a plastic tubing cutter or knife. A clean, straight cut is essential for a good connection. Slip a crimp ring onto the end of the tubing and insert the fitting. Position the crimp ring about $1/8$ to $1/4$ inch from the end of the tubing where it will be over the barbs on the fitting inside the tube.

2 Crimp the connection

Place the crimping tool jaws over the ring, making sure the ring and tool are perpendicular to the tubing. Keeping the tool and ring straight on the tubing, squeeze the handles fully closed to crimp the ring. Crimp only once; squeezing the ring several times or making a crimp in stages can result in a weak connection.

3 Connect lines

Position the mating tube and cut to length. Slip a crimp ring on the end of the tubing, slide the fitting into the tube, and crimp as in Step 2.

4 Secure and protect PEX

Secure PEX to framing with clamps above and below a fitting. Where it passes through holes in framing, add a nailing plate to protect the tubing from punctures. To terminate PEX at a fixture, install a drop-ear elbow as shown; you can attach a steel or plastic nipple or a stop valve to the elbow.

REPLACEMENTS AND UPGRADES

Quieting noisy pipes

■ **TIME:** Several hours to install an air chamber or to cushion pipes
■ **SKILLS:** Connecting pipes
■ **TOOLS:** Knife and hammer for pipe insulation, basic plumbing tools for adding an air chamber

Sudden changes in water pressure can cause pipes to vibrate, creating noise when they hit the house's framing. This page tells you what causes the noise and what you can do about it.

Water hammer is the most common pipe noise. It results from a sudden stop in the flow of water, as when you turn off a faucet. The abrupt halting of water flow creates a shock wave in the pipes, causing them to vibrate and hit against framing members.

A ticking noise can be traced to a hot water pipe that was cool, then suddenly is heated by water running through it. Pipe insulation dampens the noise. Chattering or moaning sounds may be caused by water pressure that is too high. If this is a persistent problem, call a professional to check the pressure.

DON'T BLAME PIPES

■ A machine-gun rattle, an annoying sound sometimes heard when you barely open a faucet, usually is caused by a defective seat washer.
■ Do pipes pound only when you run the dishwasher? An aging pump valve in the dishwasher creates the same rattle as a defective seat washer. Replace the pump.

Install an air chamber

Cushion hammering pipes

To eliminate pipe noises, install air chambers, also known as water-hammer arrestors, at accessible points in your supply lines. They provide a pocket of air for water to bump against. Air chambers should be installed with the closed end facing up. See page 89 for installation instructions.

Have a helper do whatever it is that causes the noise (flush the toilet or run hot water, for instance) while you search for the source of the noise. Once you find the source, see if one of the pipes has

been knocking against or rubbing a joist. Cushion the pipe at the trouble spot with pieces of foam pipe insulation (left), or use sound-insulating pipe hangers (above).

Installing a water-hammer arrestor

- **TIME:** About 2 hours
- **SKILLS:** Soldering copper pipe, connecting fittings
- **TOOLS:** Measuring tape, pipe wrenches, tubing cutter, propane torch, reaming tool, wire brush, flux brush, flux, spark lighter, solder

If you hear what sounds like banging pipes when your clothes washer (or other appliance) is at work, the noise is referred to as water hammer. Water hammer occurs when water moves through a pipe and the outlet valve is closed. The pressure created can reach 60 times that of the water moving through the pipe—upward of 600 pounds per square inch on the system. Over time, water hammer results in the failure of fittings. Many local codes require water-hammer arrestors on appliances with quick-closing valves.

1 Turn off water

Turn off the water supply at a downstream valve. Open a faucet at a lower elevation to drain the water. Mark the location for the arrestor on the pipe. Leave enough pipe to seat firmly in the new fitting. Locate the arrestor where it can point up. Some arrestors can point sideways.

2 Cut the pipe

Use a tubing cutter or hacksaw to cut the copper pipe. Make sure the cut is straight. Smooth the ends of the copper pipe using a reamer, emery cloth, and wire brush.

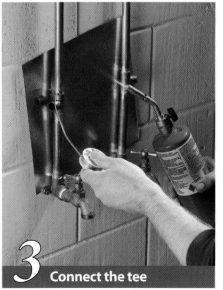

3 Connect the tee

Copper pipe must be completely dry before soldering (see page 72). Apply flux to all connecting surfaces. Assemble the connection. Make sure each pipe seats firmly in each fitting. Solder the tee to the pipe. Heat the pipe evenly with a propane torch, then apply solder (see pages 72–75).

4 Attach nipple and adapter

In tight places, place a metal sheet behind the pipe to protect surfaces. Solder a copper nipple to the tee. Connect the reducing female adapter.

5 Install the hammer arrestor

Install the threaded water-hammer arrestor and tighten by hand. Use two adjustable wrenches to tighten an additional quarter-turn.

Installing stop valves

■ **TIME:** About 2 hours to cut a pipe, install a stop valve, and run flexible line to the fixture

■ **SKILLS:** Cutting, connecting pipes

■ **TOOLS:** Hacksaw, groove-joint pliers, tubing cutter, adjustable wrench, propane torch (for copper)

Any time a water line bursts, a faucet needs repair, or a toilet needs replacing, you'll be grateful to have a stop valve in the right place. Without one, you will have to shut off the water to the entire house for even the most minor jobs, like changing a faucet washer. If you have an older home, plan to install stop valves under sinks and toilets.

No matter what the material or size of your pipes, there's a stop valve made to order. Copper lines use brass valves. Galvanized pipes typically use plated brass valves; plastic pipes, where allowed, use plastic valves. You can also use a transition fitting (see pages 68–69) to change material just prior to the stop. If the valve will be in view, choose a chrome finish.

To make the connection from a stop valve to a sink or toilet, you can use flexible copper or plastic line. Or throw away the nut and ferrule that come with the valve, and use the handy plastic or braided-metal flexible supply lines that screw on.

MATCH THE VALVE WITH THE FLEXIBLE LINE

Stop valves for sinks and toilets come with either $\frac{1}{2}$- or $\frac{3}{8}$-inch outlets. Make sure your flexible line is the same size.

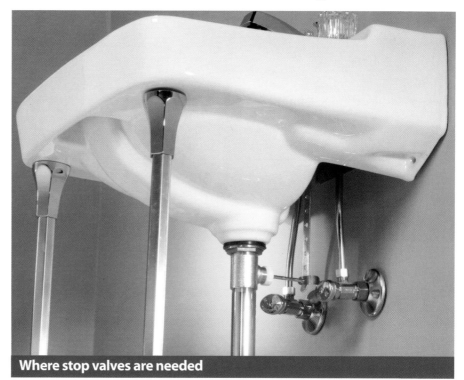

Where stop valves are needed

To determine your stop valve needs, take a look at your home's plumbing fixtures. Sinks, tubs, showers, and clothes washers require two stop valves, one each on the hot and cold lines. Toilets and water heaters require only one, on the cold water line. Dishwashers need one on the hot line only.

1 Cut pipe or tubing

Tubing cutter

In the example shown, the existing plumbing consists of galvanized pipe and flexible copper tubing. **Shut off the water supply.** Cut and remove enough tubing to make room for the valve. Leave enough supply tubing to fit the compression fitting and allow for tightening the stop valve on the steel pipe. Remove the nuts.

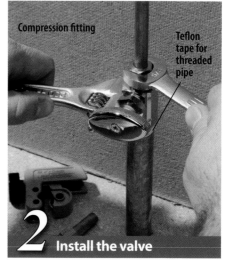

2 Install the valve

Compression fitting

Teflon tape for threaded pipe

One end of the stop valve is sized to fit regular pipe; the other receives compression-fitted flexible lines. Wrap the galvanized pipe clockwise with joint tape and install the stop valve. Slip the copper line into the other end, and tighten the compression fitting, holding the stop valve in place with a second wrench.

Installing a hand shower

- **TIME:** An hour or two for either installation
- **SKILLS:** No special skills needed
- **TOOLS:** Screwdriver, groove-joint pliers, drill, hammer, awl

A hand shower attached to an existing shower is a luxurious addition to a shower/tub area. A hand shower attached to a tub faucet is an economical alternative to installing a complete shower, sparing you the trouble of cutting open walls and installing new plumbing. A variety of designs range from the simple to the exotic. Installing one is quick and easy—a straightforward bathroom upgrade well within the skill level of any do-it-yourselfer.

At an existing shower

Shower arm

Diverter

Remove the showerhead. Tape the jaws of the pliers or wrench to protect chrome parts from scratches. Clean the threads. If your shower arm doesn't have male threads, replace it with one that does. Wrap the threads with joint tape and screw on the hand shower with pliers. The hand shower connector may have a diverter (which allows you to choose either the fixed or the handheld head), a hanger bracket (the new head fits on it), or a direct hose hookup (the hose attaches to the shower arm). For the latter, install a shower hanger (below).

Diverter valve

Shower hose fitting

A tub-only unit

To remove the old spout, insert the handle of a hammer or pliers into the spout opening and turn counterclockwise. Clean the pipe threads. You may need to remove the existing nipple and install one that is longer or shorter. Apply joint tape and screw on the new spout with a diverter valve. Attach the hose to the shower-hose fitting.

Mark screw holes

Mount the shower hanger

Some hangers have self-sticking backs. You simply peel off the paper backs and stick them in place. Be sure the wall is absolutely clean and dry before doing so. For a more permanent installation, hold the hanger in position and mark the screw holes. With a hammer and an awl or nail,

Masonry bit

Push plastic anchor in place

tap a little nick into the tile—gently, so you don't crack the tile. The nick will keep your masonry bit from slipping on the ceramic glaze as you start the hole. Drill the holes, push plastic anchors in place, and secure the hanger with screws.

Replacing a faucet

- **TIME:** Several hours to remove an old faucet and install a new one
- **SKILLS:** No special skills needed, but it may take perseverance to get the old faucet out
- **TOOLS:** Adjustable wrenches, flashlight, basin wrench, utility knife

There are thousands of styles of faucets but few variations in basic function. Kitchen faucets sometimes have sprayers and some have spouts that can rise or extend. Bathroom faucets usually include a provision for a pop-up sink drain.

There are two possibilities for supply connections: A faucet may have flexible copper supply inlets coming from the center of the unit, as shown below right, or its inlets may be located under the hot and cold handles (below left).

The hardest part of the job is physically getting at the faucet from under the sink. Clear all rags, cleaning products, and junk from the undersink cabinet. Remove cabinet doors if they are in the way, hook up a work light, and make your work area as comfortable as possible.

If you are installing a sink at the same time as the faucet, attach the faucet to the sink before you install the sink in the cabinet.

Purchase all the fixtures at once. Gather all the tools you'll use for the job. Lay all the parts and tools near the work area so whatever you're looking for is there when you need it.

The hardest part of replacing a faucet is usually removing the old faucet. Even penetrating oil may not loosen old locknuts. You may have to knock them with a hammer and screwdriver or cut them with a hacksaw.

Place a pan, bucket, or rags below the trap. Water may remain in the lines even when turned off.

Make sure thread sealants such as pipe compound, plumber's putty, silicone caulk, or joint tape are compatible with the sink fixture materials. Plumber's putty can dissolve rubber fittings and plastic parts. It also discolors cultured marble sinks.

BASIN WRENCH

A basin wrench makes removing faucet mounting and connector nuts easier. The wrench has a long handle and swivel head that reach up into the tight, cramped space. The jaws of the basin wrench automatically close around the nuts and ratchet as you turn back. The wrench can be used to tighten or loosen nuts.

Two-handle faucet

Most two-handle faucets have preassembled handles and valves. Each assembly has separate inlets to the hot and cold controls and an outlet for a sprayer.

Single-control faucet

A popular style currently is the single-control faucet with center inlets and a sprayer outlet out of the center. A variety of new styles and features include ergonomic-design pullout sprayheads that eliminate the need for a sprayer.

Stylish sinks

Kitchen side-sink fixtures need not be strictly functional. A variety of durable finishes allow you to coordinate the fixture with the sink. You can also pick up an accent color in the countertop, or strike a contrast.

Faucet fancy

Faucets all do the same thing, but they have many looks. From the range of innovative designs and cutting-edge features, you will be able to find the perfect faucet to complement your bathroom or kitchen.

1 Disconnect the water supply

Shut off the water supply to the faucets at the stop valves or the main house valve. Disconnect the supply tubes where most convenient—usually at the stop valve. To prevent twisting and kinking copper tubing or pipe, use two wrenches, one to hold the valve or fitting and the other to loosen the nut. If the nut is stuck, spray penetrating oil, as shown.

2 Remove the mounting nuts

To remove a two-handle faucet with separate inlets, as shown, use a basin wrench to loosen and remove the nuts that hold the faucet to the sink. To remove a single control faucet with copper inlets, you will likely need to remove either a center nut or two small nuts on either side. A basin wrench may do the trick, or you may need to use a screwdriver. If the faucet has a sprayer, disconnect it too.

3 Clean the sink deck

From above, lift out the faucet. Scrape the sink deck with a plastic putty knife, which will not scratch the surface. Clean away any remaining putty using a cloth dampened with paint thinner. If needed, use a mineral-deposit cleaner to complete the cleaning.

4 Seat the faucet

Insert the faucet into the sink top to test that the supply tubes fit properly through the holes. Remove the faucet and reseat it onto the sink. Some faucets have a rubber or plastic flange that seals the faucet base to the sink. Others require the application of a bead of silicone caulk or a rope of plumber's putty. Press the faucet firmly in place and check that it is centered on the sink flange.

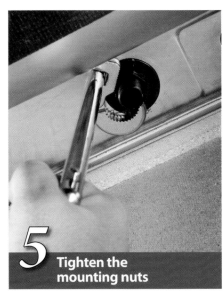

5 Tighten the mounting nuts

Have a helper hold the faucet in position while you crawl underneath to make the connections. Screw a washer and mounting nut onto each supply stem or mounting screw and tighten with a basin wrench. From above, wipe away any excess caulk or putty.

6 Connect to inlets

You may choose to wrap the threads of the inlets with joint tape. Twist the supply tube's nut onto the inlet, tightening by hand. Then use two wrenches—one to keep the inlet from twisting—to turn the nut until it seats firmly.

GETTING THE RIGHT SUPPLY TUBES

You will likely need to replace the supply tubes when you install a new faucet. When buying supply tubes, pay attention to three things: (1) Be sure to buy tubes for a faucet, not a toilet. (2) Buy tubes that fit the stop valves, which will be either $3/8$ inch or $1/2$ inch. (3) Buy tubes that are long enough to reach the new faucet's inlets, but not so long that they will create a tangle under the sink.

OTHER MOUNTING SYSTEMS

Mounting methods vary among faucets. Some one-handle faucets have a single center mounting stud, which extends slightly beyond the threaded hole. Thread a C-shape clip up onto the mounting stud (it fits around the hot and cold inlet tubes), then thread and tighten a nut to secure the clip against the bottom of the sink.

To install a two-handle faucet (as shown on page 95), connect and tighten the supply tubes to the faucet before you install it. Seat the faucet, then slip the mounting nuts up over the supply tubes and tighten them using a basin wrench.

A widespread faucet has three separate parts—two handles and one spout—which are each attached individually. Follow manufacturer's directions for hooking up the supply tubes for the handles and the spout.

7 Connect to the stop valves

Twist the supply tube's nut onto the stop valve, tightening by hand until snug. Use two wrenches—one on the nut and one holding the stop valve still—to tighten the nut. Turn on the water and test for leaks; you may need to tighten a nut a bit more firmly.

Installing a sprayer

1 Install the base

If your sprayer does not have a plastic flange to seal it to the sink, apply a bead of silicone caulk or a rope of plumber's putty to the sprayer base. Insert the sprayer hose into the hole and press down to form a good seal.

2 Tighten the mounting nut

From below, slip on the washer, then screw on and tighten the mounting nut using a basin wrench. From above, clean away any excess caulk or putty.

3 Connect the hose

Screw the sprayer hose coupling onto the faucet's diverter and tighten with a wrench. Do not overtighten. In some cases, the faucet comes without the diverter installed; you will have to install it before you connect the sprayer.

4 Install the faucet

Connect and tighten the supply tubes and seat the faucet as described on the opposite page.

5 Connect the supply lines

From below, make sure the sprayer's supply tube will not get tangled or caught on a stop valve when the sprayer is pulled out. Connect and tighten the supply tubing to the shutoff valves. Turn on the water supply and inspect for leaks.

CHECK THE INSTALLATION

Prior to turning the water on, follow these steps to prevent surprises:

- Make sure all the nuts have been tightened firmly.
- Set the faucet handle in the "off" position: Turn two-handle faucets completely off, push one-handle faucets to the down position.
- Remove the aerator or the sprayhead. Put sprayhead hoses in the sink and tie or tape them in place to prevent them from sliding out of the sink.
- Turn on the hot and cold water. Run water through the faucet for about a minute to remove debris in the lines.
- Turn off the water and install the aerator or sprayhead.
- Turn the water back on and check for leaks.

Replacing a toilet

■ **TIME:** 3 hours to remove an old toilet and install a new one
■ **SKILLS:** No special skills needed; be sure to work carefully
■ **TOOLS:** Wrenches, screwdriver, hacksaw, groove-joint pliers, putty knife

Replacing a toilet is surprisingly easy. Problems arise if the closet flange isn't at the floor surface (see box below) or if the floor isn't level (shim the toilet after you set it on the hold-down bolts).

Toilets are ceramic, so you must work carefully. A toilet will crack if hit hard or if a nut is overtightened. Most toilets sold today have the drain centered 12 inches from the back wall. Measure yours from the wall to the hold-down bolt. If it's 10 inches from the wall, buy a 10-inch toilet or install a special offset closet flange. If you need to run supply and drain lines for a new installation, see pages 117–128.

IF THE FLANGE IS LOW

If your bathroom has a new layer of flooring, the closet flange often will end up below the floor surface. In that case, a standard wax ring may not be thick enough to seal the toilet bowl to the flange. You can extend the ring upward with a special flange extender (see opposite page) or double the wax ring. Place a wax ring without a plastic flange on the toilet, then place a flanged ring on top of it.

1 Remove the old toilet

Shut off the water. Flush the toilet and remove remaining water with a sponge. Disconnect the water supply line and unscrew the hold-down nuts, which are often rusted tight. If penetrating oil fails to loosen them, cut the nuts with a hacksaw. Lift the toilet out.

Hold-down nut

Plumber's putty

Wax ring

2 Prepare the new toilet bowl

Carefully remove the new toilet bowl from its container and turn it upside down on a cushioned surface, such as a throw rug or folded drop cloth. Run a rope of plumber's putty around the perimeter of the bowl's base and fit a wax ring (sold separately) over the outlet opening.

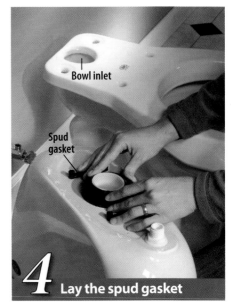

Hold-down bolt

Hold-down nut

3 Install the bowl

Return the bowl to its upright position and gently set it in place on top of the closet flange. Make sure the hold-down bolts align with the holes in the base. Press down on the bowl with both hands, and align it. Slip a metal washer and a nut over each bolt and tighten slowly. Don't overtighten—you could crack the bowl.

Bowl inlet

Spud gasket

4 Lay the spud gasket

Lay the spud gasket, beveled side down, over the bowl inlet opening. This forms the seal between the tank and the bowl. Or if you have the older-style connectors, slip the spud gasket onto the threaded tailpiece located at the bottom of the tank.

5 Install the tank

Gently lower the tank onto the bowl, aligning the tank holes with those toward the rear of the bowl. Secure the tank to the bowl with the hold-down bolts, washers, and nuts provided with the toilet. Be sure the rubber washer goes inside the tank under the bolt. Do not overtighten.

Shutoff valve

6 Attach water supply

To complete the installation, hook up the water supply line. The easiest way is to use a flexible plastic or braided supply line. Or use chrome-finished flexible copper tubing and compression fittings (see pages 77–78). Avoid kinking the tubing.

Nut — Toilet seat bolt

Install a toilet seat

To remove an old toilet seat, lower the seat and cover and pry up the little lids that cover the toilet seat bolts. Hold the nut from below, unscrew the bolts, and lift out the seat.

Clean out the area around the bolt holes. Then align the new seat with the holes and install the bolts. Screw nuts onto the bolts and tighten them just enough to firmly hold the seat.

Extending the flange

Extender ring

New tile   Flexible gasket

1 Install a flange extender

If your floor surface is more than ½ inch above the closet flange (it might be if you install new ceramic tile, for example), you must extend the flange so it's flush with the floor. Add a closet flange extender with flexible gaskets and a plastic extender ring to make up the difference. Clean off old wax, insert new bolts, and slip on a flexible gasket and the extender ring.

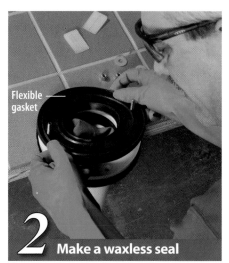

Flexible gasket

2 Make a waxless seal

The closet flange extender must fit flush with the surface of your new flooring. (If not, add an additional extender ring.) Add the second flexible gasket. This gasket takes the place of the wax ring. Most kits also include handy plastic shims for leveling the toilet once it's placed on the hold-down bolts. See page 96 for completing the bowl installation.

WATER-SAVING TOILETS

In most localities, toilets that use only 1.6 gallons of water are required for new installations. These reduce water consumption and save money, but they do not flush strongly. They differ from standard models in that they have a smaller tank or a mechanism that restricts the amount of water that enters the tank.

Don't buy a new toilet simply to save money in water use. You can reduce an old toilet's consumption by simply setting a brick into the tank or by bending the float ball's rod so the ball sits lower in the tank. Most people don't mind the reduced flushing power of new models, but if it's a problem for you, get a pressure-assisted toilet.

Replacing a gas water heater

■ **TIME:** About a day to remove an old water heater and install a new one
■ **SKILLS:** Basic plumbing skills
■ **TOOLS:** Wrenches, screwdrivers, hacksaw, groove-joint pliers, garden hose, propane torch, appliance dolly

Though water heaters sometimes last 25 years or more, they usually give out sooner—the victims of rust and sediment. When yours fails, there's no need to call in a plumber. Though it may seem like a complicated job, installing a gas water heater involves only two or three pipe hookups, and installing an electric heater requires that you connect some wires. Removing the old unit is often the most difficult part of the job.

Before you take it out, make sure your old water heater can't be fixed. If the tank itself leaks—not the pipes—the lining has rusted and the heater must be replaced. If your heater is not producing enough hot water, it may suffer from a buildup of rust and sediment, which insulates the water from the burner and forces the heater to work more often to satisfy demand. Draining the heater may flush out enough sediment to make it efficient. If it still produces too little hot water, replace the unit.

1 Drain the tank

Shut off the main water valve to your house, and shut off the gas at the heater. Drain the water lines in your home by opening hot and cold taps in an upstairs faucet. Also open both taps positioned closest to the system's lowest point. Attach a garden hose to the water heater drain valve, open the valve, and drain the tank.

2 Dismantle the flue

Remove the sheet-metal screws and dismantle enough ductwork to give yourself room to work. Keep track of which piece of ductwork goes where, and be careful not to bend it.

CAUTION

PRECAUTIONS WITH GAS

Take precautions when working with gas. If you don't have a gas shutoff near the water heater, go to your home's gas meter and shut off the gas to your house by turning the valve with a large wrench. After you turn the gas back on, be sure to relight all the pilot lights in your house.

CHOOSING THE RIGHT WATER HEATER

Check the nameplate on the old unit, and note its capacity. It's safe to purchase a new one of the same size, unless you have recently installed or plan to buy an appliance that consumes a lot of hot water, such as a dishwasher. A 30- to 50-gallon unit is usually large enough for a home.

Units designed to heat water quickly, called fast recovery units, are more expensive to buy and operate, but they handle peak demand times better. Standard units heat more slowly but are more economical.

If you have an electric water heater and hard water, consider a unit with an extra anode for collecting mineral deposits (see the drawing on page 40).

3 Disconnect the gas line

Many localities require that the gas line must be rigid pipe all the way to the water heater; others allow you to use a flexible gas line. Take apart a gas line union (as shown), or disconnect the flexible line.

If you need to, shim at base for plumb.

4 Disconnect the water lines

Mark hot and cold water lines to prevent hooking up the new heater backward. For galvanized pipe, open unions near the unit. For rigid copper, cut the pipe with a hacksaw or tubing cutter just below the shutoff valves. Make the cuts straight so you can tap into the lines easily with new soldered pipe or flexible water lines when you install the new heater. If you have flexible lines, disconnect them. Move the old unit out with an appliance dolly.

5 Set the new unit in place

Move the new water heater into place. Position it to make the gas and water connections as easy as possible. Check for plumb and level, shimming the unit if necessary. If the area is prone to dampness, place the new water heater in a traylike base, available at home centers.

6 Connect the water lines

Check code requirements for the water lines. If they're permitted, flexible copper water connectors are usually the easiest way to go. Otherwise you'll have to solder rigid copper or install galvanized pipe with a union. To save energy, install heat-saver nipples at each inlet. These temperature-sensitive in-line valves hold back water until it's needed. Follow directions, installing the cold water nipple with the arrow pointing down and the hot water nipple with the arrow pointing up.

CAUTION

LIFT WITH CARE

If sediment buildup clogged your old heater, it will be extremely heavy. Enlist a helper and have a good appliance dolly available. Take care not to strain your back.

INSTALLING A RELIEF VALVE

You may have to purchase a temperature-and-pressure-relief valve separately. Be sure it matches the working-pressure rating of the tank, as given on the nameplate. Wrap the threads with joint tape, and screw in the valve—either on top or near the top on the side.

Replacing a gas water heater *(continued)*

Burner control

7 Hook up the gas

Connect a gas (black pipe) nipple to the burner control of the water heater and connect the nipple to the gas line. Be sure to install a drip leg to collect sediment and moisture from the gas line.

8 Install the flue

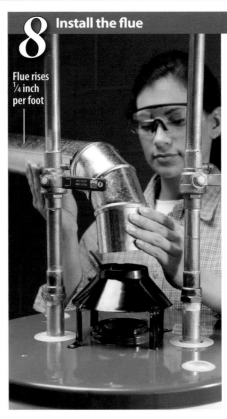

Flue rises ¼ inch per foot

If your old flue worked well and your new water heater is the same height as the old one, you can reuse the old flue. Make sure it's clear; clean out any dust, rust, or sediment. If you replace or add to the vent, use galvanized pipe fittings that are designed for venting gas. When running a horizontal section, maintain at least a ¼-inch-per-foot rise. Insert male ends of the vent into female ends away from the water heater so the fumes will not have a chance to escape. Fasten each joint of the vent with two sheet-metal screws.

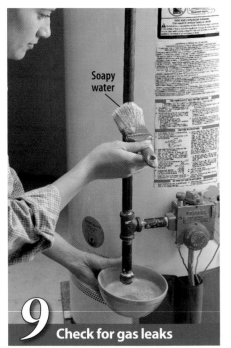

Soapy water

9 Check for gas leaks

Open the gas stop valve. Test for leaks by brushing soapy water on all the connections. Watch for bubbles. If you see any, tighten the connection. If they persist, shut off the gas, disassemble, carefully clean the threads, and start again.

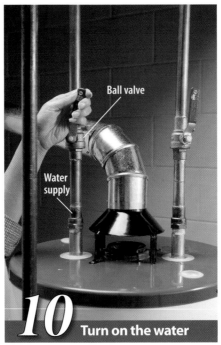

Ball valve

Water supply

10 Turn on the water

Open the water supply valve. Open the nearest hot water faucet about halfway and allow the system to bleed. Air will come out first, then the spattering of water mixed with air. When the water flows freely, close the faucet.

11 Light the pilot

Open the access panel at the bottom of the tank and light the pilot according to the directions printed on the water heater. Adjust the temperature setting; water heated to not more than 120°F is best in most situations.

Replacing an electric water heater

- **TIME:** About 1 day
- **SKILLS:** Making electrical and plumbing connections
- **TOOLS:** Wrenches for unions or flexible fittings, garden hose for draining, level, appliance dolly, screwdriver, voltage tester

Installing an electric water heater is similar to installing a gas unit. The differences are that you make electrical rather than gas connections, and an electric water heater has no flue.

CAUTION

DANGER! HIGH VOLTAGE
Working with 240-volt circuits is a serious matter. Remove the fuse or turn off the circuit breaker, and check to make sure the power is off.

1 Remove the panel and test

Shut off the power and water. Remove the access panel for the thermostat (usually behind the lower panel), push aside any insulation, and lift or remove the plastic guard. Test for current with a voltage tester to make sure the circuit is off.

2 Disconnect, mark wires

Remove the electrical cover plate at the side or the top of the unit. Disconnect the wires and mark them so you'll know where to attach them on the new unit. Loosen the cable clamp and carefully pull the cable out.

Complete Steps 1, 4, and 5 on pages 98–99.

3 Connect water pipes

Connect water lines (see page 99). Supply lines can be galvanized steel pipe (see pages 80–81), rigid copper (see pages 72–75), or flexible water connectors. Install a ball valve on the supply line. Install a relief valve and attach an outlet pipe (see page 99).

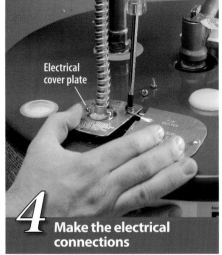

4 Make the electrical connections

Remove the electrical cover plate. Run the cable through the clamp. Connect the black and white wires with wire connectors and attach the ground wire to the ground screw. Tighten the screw on the clamp to hold the cable in place, gently push the wires inside, and replace the cover plate.

5 Set the thermostat

Adjust the temperature setting; water heated to not more than 120°F is best in most situations. Press the reset button and replace the plastic guard, insulation, and access panels. Turn the water on as shown in Step 10 on page 100.

Installing a garbage disposer

■ **TIME:** Several hours, not including the electrical receptacle and switch
■ **SKILLS:** Making basic electrical and plumbing connections
■ **TOOLS:** Hammer, spud wrench, screwdriver, groove-joint pliers, putty knife, wire stripper

A garbage disposer is a useful kitchen upgrade that is fairly simple to install. The hardest part is working under your sink, so pad the cabinet with plenty of towels to make it comfortable. If you're installing a new sink, attach the disposer to the sink first, then set the sink in place.

SELF-SWITCHING DISPOSER

Most disposers require a switched receptacle, leaving the homeowner with the difficult job of finding a good location for the switch. A wall switch requires you to fish an electrical line up the wall above the countertop. Another option is to place the switch on the face of the lower cabinets, but that puts it within the reach of children. Consider spending the extra money for a self-switching garbage disposer. Plugged into a regular receptacle, it turns on when food is pushed into it.

1 Supply electricity

If necessary, install an electrical box under the sink near the disposer. Install a GFCI receptacle. Or you can hardwire the disposer (see Step 6 on the opposite page and refer to the manufacturer's instructions). Unless you are using a self-switching disposer, install a switch as well.

Basket strainer

Detach tailpiece of trap from bottom of strainer

2 Remove the basket strainer

Disconnect the trap assembly from the basket strainer and the drainpipe. Remove the locknut that holds the strainer using a spud wrench or a hammer and screwdriver. Lift out the strainer and clean old putty from the opening using a putty knife, paint thinner, and an abrasive pad.

3 Install the mounting assembly

Gasket

Mounting rings   Flange   Snap ring

Remove excess putty after tightening

First take apart the mounting assembly. To do this, remove the snap ring, mounting rings, and gasket from the flange. Then lay a rope of putty around the sink opening and seat the flange in the opening. Have a helper hold the flange in place as you work from underneath. Slip the gasket, mounting rings, and snap ring onto the flange. The snap ring will keep the mounting assembly in place temporarily. Tighten the mounting assembly against the sink by turning the screws counterclockwise. Tighten each screw a little at a time to assure a solid seal. With a putty knife, shave away excess putty.

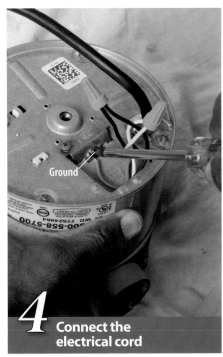

4 Connect the electrical cord

Ground

Remove the disposer's electrical cover plate. Strip sheathing and wire insulation from an approved appliance cord and insert the cord into the opening. Tighten the clamp while holding the cord in place. Make the electrical connections in the disposer, gently push the wires into place, and reinstall the cover plate.

Dishwasher drain nipple

Drain elbow

5 Attach the disposer

Secure the drain elbow to the disposer. If you'll drain a dishwasher through the unit, remove the knockout inside the nipple. To mount the disposer, lift it into place and rotate it until it engages and tightens. (This may take some muscle.) Once the connection is made, rotate the disposer to the best position for attaching the drain lines.

6 Make the electrical connection

Shut off power. If you installed an electrical receptacle, simply insert the disposer's plug. For a hardwired installation, connect black (hot) and white (neutral) wires in the box to the hot and neutral disposer leads in accordance with the manufacturer's instructions. Connect ground wires.

Dishwasher drain nipple

Dishwasher drain elbow

Slip nuts

Trap

7 Connect the drain

Fit a slip nut and a rubber washer onto the drain elbow and fasten the trap to the elbow and the drainpipe. You may need to cut the elbow to make the connection. For double sinks, connect the elbow to the second bowl drain. If you will be draining a dishwasher through the disposer, connect the dishwasher drain hose to the drain nipple of the disposer. Use an automotive clamp to attach the hose, tightening it in place with a screwdriver or ratchet and socket. Run water down through the disposer to test for leaks. Turn the electrical power back on. With standing water in the bowl, turn the disposer on and make sure it is securely attached.

TIPS ON INSTALLING THE DRAINPIPES

With a double-bowl sink, it's possible to remove the disposer's drain elbow and run pipe straight to the trap of the other bowl. It's better, however, to install a separate trap for the disposer so each bowl has its own trap.

If the original drain traps are in good condition, reuse them. In most cases, if you buy one extension piece, you will have enough material to complete the piping. If your old trap looks at all worn, replace it while you have everything apart.

Installing a dishwasher

- **TIME:** About 2 hours to replace; a full day or more for a new installation
- **SKILLS:** Simple electrical and plumbing skills for replacing, plus carpentry skills for a new installation
- **TOOLS:** Drill, electrical tools, carpentry tools, screwdriver, groove-joint pliers

Replacing an old dishwasher with a new one is a fairly simple job. Most units fit neatly into a 24-inch-wide undercounter cavity, and all are prewired and ready for simple supply, drain, and electrical hookups. Installing a new dishwasher, however, is a much larger job: You must make room for it in the cabinetry and bring in electrical, supply, and drain lines.

To avoid straining the discharge pump, position the dishwasher as near to the sink as possible.

1 Prepare the opening

Shut off the water and shut off the electrical power. If you are replacing an existing dishwasher, remove its lower panel and disconnect the supply line, the drain hose, and the electrical line. Remove screws that attach it to the countertop and carefully pull out the unit.

To make a new installation, remove a 24-inch-wide base cabinet or build a space to fit the dishwasher. Bore a hole large enough to allow for the supply and drain lines near the lower back of the side panel of the adjoining cabinet. The dishwasher will need its own 15- or 20-amp circuit. Run a circuit from the service panel (you may want to hire a licensed electrician to install this).

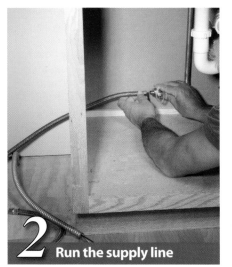

2 Run the supply line

Cut into the hot water supply line and insert a standard tee fitting, a nipple, and a shutoff valve. Run flexible copper tubing into the cavity, leaving enough line to reach the dishwasher supply fitting. (See pages 72–86 for information on working with various types of pipes.)

3 Provide drain fittings

You can drain the dishwasher either into the sink drain or into a garbage disposer, if you have one.

For sink drainage, install a dishwasher tailpiece. Loosen the slip nuts and remove the tailpiece, insert the dishwasher tailpiece into the trap, and cut the old tailpiece to fit above it. Connect all the pieces and tighten the slip nuts.

To drain a dishwasher into a garbage disposer, use a screwdriver and hammer to remove the metal knockout inside the drain nipple located near the top of the disposer. The knockout, when freed, may fall into the grinding chamber of the disposer—be sure to take it out.

4 Attach the drain line

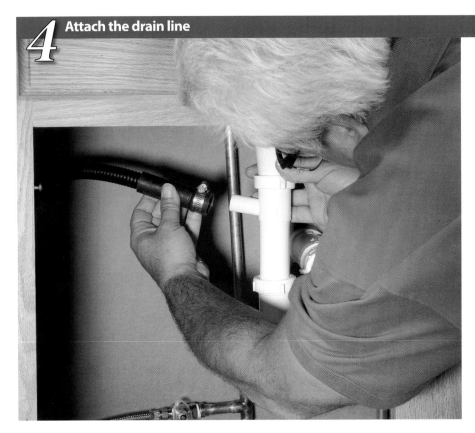

Thread the drain line through the hole in the cabinet and slip it onto the dishwasher tailpiece or drain nipple—you may have to push hard. Secure it with an automotive hose clamp.

To ensure proper operation of the appliance, the drain line must make a loop, so that at some point it is raised near the height of the countertop. The drain line will vibrate during use, so wrap a couple of lengths of wire around it and fasten them to screws driven into the underside of the countertop. Take care that the screws do not poke through the countertop.

Some local codes require an air gap at the top of the loop. You can place this in a knockout hole in the sink or drill a hole for it in the countertop. Run one line from the drain nipple to the air gap and another from the air gap to the dishwasher drain outlet.

5 Make the hookups

Position the ends of the water supply line, drain line, and electrical cable approximately at the locations where they will connect to the dishwasher. Remove the bottom cover plate from the dishwasher and slide the unit carefully into place, watching to make sure the lines are not damaged. Make sure the dishwasher is all the way in position.

Tighten the compression nut and drain line clamp firmly and make secure electrical connections.

Turn the leg's leveling screws to level the dishwasher. Anchor the dishwasher to the underside of the countertop with screws. Turn on the water and the electrical power. Before reattaching access panels, run the washer and watch for leaks.

Installing a hot water dispenser

- **TIME:** About 3 hours, not including installation of an electrical receptacle
- **SKILLS:** Drilling, handling of flexible line, electrical skills
- **TOOLS:** Drill, hole saw or metal-boring hole saw, screwdriver, groove-joint pliers, wire strippers

This appliance gives you an immediate source of piping hot water for instant soup, tea, and coffee, or for quick blanching of vegetables.

Installation is relatively simple. The most difficult step is adding an electrical receptacle under the sink. You typically can't use the garbage disposer's receptacle because it works on a switch, and this one must be live all the time.

When you open the faucet valve, unheated water enters the dispenser through the supply tube, warming as it passes through the expansion chamber. The pressure of the incoming water forces hot water from the holding tank and expansion chamber (where it cools to 200°F) out the spout. When the temperature in the tank drops, a thermostat activates heating elements to return the water to the set temperature.

MAINTAINING YOUR HOT WATER DISPENSER

- With a dispenser installed, water may drip from the spout even when the valve is off. If this happens, lower the thermostat setting—pressure from water that is too hot can force water past the valve.
- If you're not going to use the dispenser for a period of time, unplug it or switch it off, close off the water supply valve, and drain the unit of water.
- Take care when you use your dispenser—the water is indeed hot. Instruct children not to use it. Be sure to keep flammable items such as shopping bags and rags well away from the holding tank under the sink.

CAUTION

CHECK THE CIRCUIT

Any heating element draws a lot of current. If a circuit is already overloaded, you need to have an electrician install a grounded circuit for this unit. If your unit has a plug, be sure to install a ground fault circuit interrupter (GFCI) receptacle as well.

Expansion chamber

Faucet valve

Water supply tube

Insulation

Holding tank

Heating elements

1 Wire a receptacle

If necessary, install a grounded electrical receptacle that is always live under the sink, near the dispenser location. Most building codes require a GFCI receptacle within 6 feet of a water source.

2 Drill a hole

Decide where you want to place the dispenser. If you have a stainless-steel sink, you can buy a hole saw designed to cut through metal. Drill slowly. (If you are installing a new sink, select one with an extra hole.)

Your sink may have a knockout hole. If it's the right size, just punch the insert out from below.

It may be easier to drill a hole near the back edge of the countertop near the sink, using a fine-tooth hole saw. Make sure you leave room for the entire diameter of the unit. Position the hole so the faucet is close enough to run into the sink.

3 Attach the faucet assembly

Insert the assembly with its gasket into the hole. You may need a helper to hold the dispenser in the correct position as you crawl underneath and work. Slip on the washer, screw on the mounting nut, and tighten firmly.

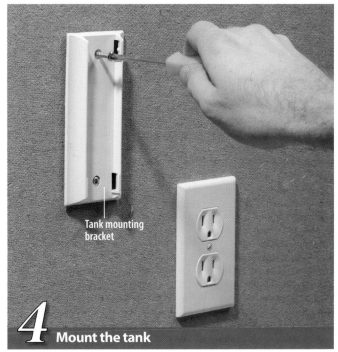

Tank mounting bracket

4 Mount the tank

Place the tank mounting bracket 12 to 14 inches below the underside of the countertop, and make sure it's plumb before fastening it with screws. Mount the tank onto the bracket.

Hot water line — Water line to dispenser — Hot water line — Shutoff valve — Saddle-tee valve — Tee — Nipple — Adapter ring — Water line to dispenser

5 Install water supply valve

Shut off the water and drain the line. To supply the unit with water, tap into the hot water line that serves the sink. If codes permit, use a saddle-tee valve. Don't use the puncture-type saddle tee. Although it is simpler to install, it clogs easily. Instead drill a small hole in the supply line, then secure the clamp to the line.

If saddle tees are not permitted in your locality, break into the line (see pages 122–123) and install a standard tee fitting. Add a nipple and a shutoff valve. Use an adapter fitting to make the transition to a flexible water line that matches your dispenser's supply line.

Incoming water supply

6 Connect the lines

Secure the two longer tubes to the tank assembly and the shorter one to the water supply tube, using a compression nut and ferrule on each threaded fitting. The longer tubes are coded to prevent confusion. Restore water pressure and check for leaks. Let the tank fill before plugging in or turning on the unit.

Replacing a sump pump

- **TIME:** Half a day to a full day
- **SKILLS:** Working with and connecting plastic fittings, drilling
- **TOOLS:** Keyhole saw, power drill, caulking gun, screwdriver, level

A sump pump assists in removing water from a wet basement, transforming it into usable space. But before you run out and buy a sump pump, first identify the source of water in the basement. If water seeps into your basement because of a high water table, removing the water with a sump pump is the answer.

When water enters the basement through leaking foundation walls, explore options to seal the basement and transport the outside water away from the foundation. Also check the external perimeter around the foundation. Soil should slope away, carrying surface water into the yard. If not, build up the soil level. It will help direct water away from the basement.

A $1/3$-horsepower sump pump will meet the needs of most homes. Consider a $1/2$-horsepower pump if a $1/3$-horsepower pump will not keep up with the water. Determining the size needed depends on the area of drainage connected to the sump, the depth to groundwater, the basement depth, and other factors. Rather than going through calculations, talk to your home center or hardware retailer about which pump best meets your need.

If you are simply replacing a sump pump, you most likely will not have to run a new discharge pipe.

AVOID AN ENDLESS CYCLE

When installing a discharge pipe through the foundation, add enough length to carry the water away from the foundation. Dumping too close to the foundation may result in the water finding its way back into the sump pit. This just creates an endless cycle. Ideally, water should be discharged at least 20 feet from the house. This is not always possible in a residential area. Use common sense. Be careful not to discharge onto a neighbor's lot or septic drainage field.

1 Remove the old sump pump

Unplug the power cord for the sump pump. If the cord is taped to the discharge pipe, remove the tape, freeing the cord. There should be a rubber coupling with clamps that connects the sump pump to a check valve and to the discharge line. Disconnect the clamps and remove the rubber coupling. Inspect the coupling for damage and replace it, if necessary. Lift the old sump pump out of the pit.

2 Assemble the new sump pump

Determine the placement of the new sump pump and measure the lengths needed for the discharge piping. The sump pump and the discharge fitting are not normally preassembled, so you will need to put them together. Follow the manufacturer's assembly instructions.

3 Set pump in the pit

Position the pump so the float is a couple of inches below the floor surface. The sump pump requires a solid base that will withstand water and prevent the pump from moving. Tamp the gravel. If the base is still not solid, stabilize the pump with a small brick or piece of concrete. Do not use wood.

4 Check that it's level

Use a small torpedo level to make sure the pump housing is level and that the discharge pipe is plumb. If necessary, adjust the discharge pipe and shim the housing with plastic shims. Do not use wood shims.

5 Connect the discharge line

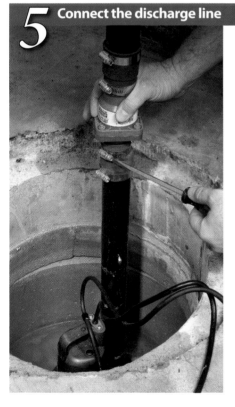

Position a rubber coupling on the check valve. Place two hose clamps over the rubber coupling. Slide one clamp over the check valve and tighten. Slide the other clamp over the sump pump discharge pipe and tighten it. If you don't have a check valve on the discharge line, install one to prevent water from backing up into the sump pump. Run the power cord along the discharge pipe, fastening it to the pipe with electrician's tape. Adjust the float to the level recommended by the manufacturer. Plug the pump cord into a nearby GFCI-protected receptacle. Pour a 5-gallon bucket of water into the sump pit to test it.

PVC VS. ABS

When installing discharge pipe, some codes allow you to use either PVC or ABS. One disadvantage with ABS is that it tends to become brittle over time and then is susceptible to cracking. Check your local codes before using ABS.

CAUTION

DON'T DISCHARGE INTO THE SEPTIC SYSTEM

Never discharge a sump pump into a septic system, sewer drain, or floor drain. During wet conditions the septic system drainage field is typically saturated trying to handle the normal flow of wastewater. The discharge from a sump pump can damage the septic system and kill the bacteria necessary to digest the waste.

Installing an undersink filter

■ **TIME:** Usually 30 minutes
■ **SKILLS:** Basic plumbing skills
■ **TOOLS:** Tubing cutter, flashlight, screwdriver

A whole-house filtration system will supply you with filtered water in every tap and likely will prolong the life of your water-using appliances. But because it is fairly difficult to install and requires regular filter changes, most homeowners opt to go without. They reason that most water does not need to be treated because it is used for bathing, flushing away waste, and washing clothes. Instead, they choose to filter the water that counts most: their drinking and cooking water.

You can install a unit that gives you filtered water every time you turn on the cold water at your kitchen sink, or you can install a separate faucet with the filter. The first type saves you the trouble of drilling a hole and installing a separate faucet. The separate faucet (installed much like the hot water dispenser on page 106) means you'll change filter cartridges less often.

Some systems include an activated-charcoal filter. This two-canister system takes more time to install but adds another filtration stage.

Before you purchase a unit, measure the space under your sink to make sure the new unit will fit. The connectors for the various types available are fairly simple, ranging from standard compression fittings to simple connectors designed to quickly attach to flexible supply lines. In most cases, you need only shut off the cold-water supply, cut into a flexible supply, and install the system.

1 Place filter near cold water line

Anchor the filter in a location that's easy to access when it's time to replace the filter cartridge. Allow enough clearance underneath to unscrew the canister. Use the screws provided to fasten it to the cabinet back or wall. If you don't have a flexible cold-water supply line, install one. Cut into the cold-water supply using a tubing cutter or plastic tubing cutter.

2 Hook up the filter

Note which filter inlet is marked for the incoming supply and connect that flexible tube to the section of supply line nearest the shutoff valve. Connectors vary. For the ones shown, simply push the tubing in and they're joined. Connect the tube that carries filtered water to the flexible supply line for the faucet. Follow the manufacturer's directions for operation and maintenance.

Plumbing an icemaker

- **TIME:** Usually 30 minutes
- **SKILLS:** Basic plumbing skills
- **TOOLS:** Tubing cutter, adjustable wrench, flashlight, screwdriver, drill and bits

If you have just purchased a new refrigerator with an icemaker, the appliance dealer may offer installation for a minimal cost. If not, installing an icemaker yourself is usually not a difficult project.

If you would like to add an icemaker to an older refrigerator, contact an appliance dealer to see if you can buy and install a retrofit unit.

If you have hard or bad-tasting water, consider installing a small water filter for the icemaker. You will likely need to change the filter cartridge once a year or so.

Use copper tubing, as shown on this page, or plastic tubing. Plastic is less likely to kink, making it a good choice if you plan to move the refrigerator often. However, plastic tubing clogs more easily than copper tubing.

Here we show installing a saddle-tee valve, which is usually reliable. For a sturdier installation, you may choose to install a stop valve instead.

Twist handle clockwise to seat valve

1 Install a saddle-tee valve

Find a cold-water pipe that is near the refrigerator and that can be accessed for future maintenance. There are two types of saddle valves. (See "Saddle Valves," below right.) Determine which type you have, and install it accordingly.

2 Run the tubing

Purchase plenty of tubing, so you can run it around in gentle curves and provide loops that allow the refrigerator to be moved in and out. On the floor behind the refrigerator and near the base molding, use a drill with a long bit to bore a hole through to the basement or crawlspace below. Or drill a hole near the bottom of a wall to reach an adjacent room. Carefully uncoil the tubing; if it kinks, the whole piece must be replaced. Thread the tubing through the hole and run it to the saddle valve. Behind the refrigerator, leave several coils of tubing. Take care not to squeeze a tubing end, or it will not fit into the compression fitting.

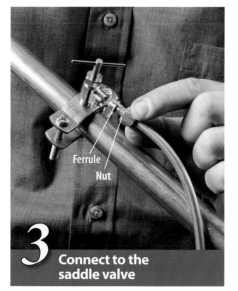

Ferrule
Nut

3 Connect to the saddle valve

Bend the tubing so its end will run straight into the saddle valve's fitting. Slip on a nut and a ferrule, poke the tubing in, and tighten the nut.

4 Connect to the refrigerator

Place the other end of the tubing in a bucket and turn on the saddle valve. Run water for a minute or so to purge the line of debris. Turn off the saddle-tee valve. At the refrigerator's icemaker connection, attach the tubing as you did at the saddle valve (Step 3). Open the saddle valve and check for leaks; you may need to tighten a nut.

SADDLE VALVES

There are two types of saddle valves. A self-punching saddle valve drives a spike that punctures the copper water supply pipe, allowing you to add the new water line without shutting off the water supply. Simply clamp it in place and twist the valve handle until the spike punctures the pipe.

The second type requires you to drill a hole through the water supply line, twist the valve into the hole, and clamp it to the water pipe. You must shut off the water to install this type.

Choosing a water softener

A water softener removes minerals (especially iron, calcium, and magnesium) from water by means of ion exchange. As water passes through the unit, minerals are absorbed and replaced with sodium, which comes from salt that you must add to the storage tank from time to time.

The resulting soft water cleans clothes better than mineral-laden hard water, which creates fewer suds. The drawback is that it adds salt to the water—probably not enough to damage your health, but enough to affect the taste of the water.

It is best to have a cold-water bypass so some faucets receive unsoftened cold water. At least make sure your toilets and outside sill cocks do not receive softened water, or you will be paying for a lot of extra salt.

In most cases, it pays to have a water softener service install and maintain your water softener. If you were to install one yourself, you would have to make drain and electrical connections, then periodically flush and recharge your system. With a service unit, the dealer simply brings a fresh tank and takes the old one to regenerate it.

In the unit shown, a bypass valve lets you or the dealer service the unit without shutting down your home's water supply.

FILTERING BACTERIA

If bacteria in the water are a problem rather than simply minerals, sediment, taste, or odor, choose a filter carefully. Some filters actually increase the amount of bacteria in your drinking water because they remove chlorine. Bacteria can grow in dechlorinated water if it sits for a while, even if it's in your refrigerator.

Installing a water softener

- **TIME:** 4 to 6 hours
- **SKILLS:** Working with copper pipe, using basic plumbing tools, connecting fittings
- **TOOLS:** Adjustable wrench, screwdriver, tape measure, solder, flux, propane torch, deburring tool, emery cloth

Water that is "hard" is laced with minerals such as calcium and iron. Hard water inhibits the cleaning power of soap and detergent and also makes rinsing difficult, so you end up with soapy buildup in sinks and tubs. It creates reddish iron stains or collections of white mineral deposits, which can clog faucets and pipes.

Through a process called ion exchange, a water softener removes most of the minerals and replaces them with trace amounts of sodium salt. The resulting water cleans well and will not harm plumbing, but it may taste bad.

If you have hard water, it is a neighborhood-wide problem (unless you get your water from your own well). Consult with a plumbing expert at a local hardware store or home center to find the best solution.

The easiest option is to have a water softener company install and maintain a softener. However, you can save money if you install one yourself. Maintenance involves periodically adding salt and cleaning a line and a screen.

You can install a water softener on the main water supply line where it enters your house. Or, install it on the hot-water pipe that leaves the water heater; that way, your cold water will taste better.

1 Assemble and position the softener

Place the water softener near the main supply line or a hot-water pipe, in a spot where you can easily reach it for adding salt. Follow manufacturer's instructions for assembling the unit. Attach the drain hose and the overflow tube, and run them to a point that is at least 1½ inches above a floor drain or a utility tub drain. Check that the softener is stable and level; you may need to shim the bottom of the unit.

2 Install the bypass valve

The softener comes with a bypass valve, which you must assemble and install. In most cases, you simply slip on O-rings, push the valves into the ports, and attach the valves with push-on clips. Be sure to lubricate the O-rings as recommended by the manufacturer.

Turn off the water at the main house supply valve (or to the pipe you are breaking into), and open a nearby faucet to drain the line. Shut off gas or electricity to the water heater.

3 Connect the water supply

Near the water softener, break into the supply pipe. Remove a section of pipe about 5 inches long. Install elbows and pipes that reach to the bypass valves. The valves typically accept ¾-inch pipe. If the pipe is larger, use reducer couplings or reducer elbows to make the transition. Local codes may require that you configure the pipes so that the water can bypass the softener when repairs are needed. This typically involves using tees rather than elbows, and installing three shutoff valves.

Do all your soldering while the pipe is not touching the bypass valves, or you could damage them. Run copper pipes down into the bypass valves. The final connection is usually made using a coupler supplied by the manufacturer.

Remove aerators and showerheads throughout the house, and run water for several minutes. Turn off the faucets and replace the aerators and heads. Follow the manufacturer's instructions for programming the softener.

113

Installing a water filtration system

If you receive municipal water, you'll find information concerning water quality at city hall. If you have a well, you're on your own. Your local department of health can recommend a company to test your water to see if you need a filter. A test for bacteria is relatively inexpensive, but a full test that includes a search for pesticides, organic matter, and other potential problems is costly. Ask local officials if other people in your area have had similar tests done and what, if any, contaminants were found.

If the taste of your drinking water is your major concern, try a faucet filter before you get involved with a more expensive installation. If you have mineral-laden hard water, install a water softener (see pages 112–113).

WATER FILTRATION OPTIONS	
Sediment	This option uses a filter to screen out particles that clog your aerators and make your water look cloudy. Usually a sediment filter is used in conjunction with an activated-charcoal filter.
Activated charcoal	This filter removes organic chemicals and pesticides. If your water is heavily chlorinated, it will remove much of the chlorine and improve the taste of your water. If taste is your major concern, install a unit at the kitchen spout. Whole-house units require you to change the charcoal filter fairly frequently.
Reverse osmosis	This is the most extreme measure, capable of removing bacteria and harmful chemicals. It is expensive and bulky and requires at least one holding tank. You can combine this system with an activated-charcoal system installed near the kitchen sink.
Water softener	Also called an ion-exchange unit, this system greatly reduces minerals such as calcium and iron. Requires periodic flushing and addition of salt.

Installing a whole-house system

- **TIME:** Half a day
- **SKILLS:** Good plumbing skills
- **TOOLS:** Wrenches and pliers; propane torch, if you need to solder copper pipe

The typical whole-house system shown at right combines a sediment filter with an activated-charcoal unit. The plumbing is not complicated, but you'll have to shut off water to the whole house before beginning. You also may have to reroute or raise pipes in order to gain enough room to install the two units.

Whole-house water filter

Shut off the water and drain the line. At a convenient point near the outlet side of the water meter (or just inside the house, if you have no meter), break into the line by opening a union or cutting the pipe (see pages 122–123). Install a shutoff valve if you don't have one (see page 90).

Remove 4 feet of pipe and work toward the meter. If you wish, add a stop valve to cut off backflow when you need to change filters. Then install the charcoal filter, a nipple, and finally the sediment filter. Tighten all joints, then make the last joint with a union or sleeve coupling.

Planning for new fixtures

Most improvements shown in this book are add-ons, those that connect new fittings or fixtures to existing pipes. Running new lines requires an understanding of how supply, drain, and vent pipes work in general and detailed knowledge of your home's plumbing system.

New supply lines are the easiest to plan. They require no slope or venting, just the correct pipe size (see box below). You can run them almost anywhere you need them.

Far trickier are the drain-waste-vent (DWV) lines that carry away water, waste, and gases. The illustrations at right and on page 116 show straightforward ways to accommodate a new fixture. Your situation may be more complex and may require professional planning and installation.

For a new installation, even a minor one, you'll have to apply to your local building department for a permit. Be sure to arrange to have the work checked by the building inspector before you cover up new pipes.

SIZING SUPPLY LINES

Check with your local building department for the size of the supply line required. As a general rule, most departments require that a line supplying one or two fixtures be ½ inch. Lines that supply three or more fixtures must be at least ¾ inch.

Planning drain lines

The first step in planning an extension to your plumbing system is to map out exactly where existing lines run. Your home probably has a drainage arrangement similar to the one shown. Notice that some of the fixtures (toilet, double sink) cluster near a wet wall, which contains the main stack. A wet wall is usually a few inches thicker than other walls to accommodate the 3- or 4-inch-diameter stack that runs up through the roof. (One way to find a wet wall is to note the location of the stack on the roof.)

The fixtures drain directly into the main stack or into horizontal runs that slope downward at a pitch of at least ¼ inch per running foot. Fixtures more than a few feet from the stack (such as the bathtub and bathroom sink) must be vented with a loop that goes up and back to the stack. Called a revent or circuit vent, this branch is concealed inside walls and floors of normal thickness. Fixtures even farther away (such as the shower and utility sink) may require a separate stack. Requirements vary on revents and new vents, so check local codes.

Position the new fixtures as close as possible to an existing stack to minimize necessary wall damage.

Venting fixtures

Think of a main stack as a two-way chimney: Water and wastes go down; gases go up. Just as you wouldn't install a fireplace without a chimney, neither should you consider adding a fixture without properly venting it. Strangle the air supply of a drain, and you risk creating a siphoning effect that sucks water out of traps. This, in turn, breaks the seal that provides protection from gas backup—and often retards the flow of wastes as well.

Codes specifically state how you must vent fixtures. These requirements differ from one locality to another, so check your community's regulations for details about the systems shown here.

With unit venting—sometimes referred to as common venting—two similar fixtures share the same stack fitting. This method allows you to put a new fixture back-to-back with one that already exists. The fixtures are installed on opposite sides of the wet wall. To install a unit vent, open up the wall, replace the existing sanitary tee with a sanitary cross, and connect both traps to it. The drains of unit-vented fixtures must be set at equal heights.

Wet venting uses a section of one fixture's drain line to double as the vent for another. Some codes forbid wet venting. Those that allow it often specify that the vertical drain must be at least one pipe size larger than the upper fixture drain. In no case can the vertical drain be smaller than the lower drain.

Regardless of how you vent a fixture, codes limit the distance between the trap outlet and the vent. These distances depend on the size of the drain line you're running. For 1¼-, 1½-, and 2-inch drain lines—the sizes you'll most likely be working with—2, 3, and 5 feet, respectively, are typical distances. (If you're adding plastic drain line, see page 124. For how to tap into a cast-iron drain, see page 125.)

Often the best way to install a new fixture is with a revent, or circuit vent, but clear this with your local building department before you decide to do it. Some codes forbid you to use this solution with heavy-use items such as toilets or showers.

Sometimes the only solution is to install a separate vent that runs through the roof (see pages 126–127). If the fixture will be installed on the top floor, it'll be relatively simple.

UNIT VENTING
(common venting)

Sanitary cross

Sanitary tee

WET VENTING

REVENTING
(circuit venting)

SEPARATE VENTING

New vent

Sanitary tee

Roughing in sinks, tubs, showers, and toilets

- **TIME:** Roughly 2 days to cut walls and rough in a sink, toilet, and tub or shower
- **SKILLS:** Basic plumbing and carpentry skills
- **TOOLS:** Reciprocating saw, basic plumbing tools, basic carpentry tools

Plan the location of your bathroom fixtures carefully: A few inches one way or the other make the difference between a bathroom that is comfortable and one that feels cramped and inconvenient.

First map the floor of your bathroom on a piece of graph paper. Then cut out small-scale pieces of paper to represent the fixtures. Move the pieces until you find the most usable configuration. If a door opens inward, make sure it swings completely without hitting a fixture.

The dimensions given in the drawings at right show the minimum requirements for ease of use. Do not place fixtures closer to each other than specified. Once you decide on your floor plan, use masking tape or a carpenter's pencil to mark your floors and walls for the rough-in dimensions, using the diagrams below right.

If you are remodeling a room that you don't want to mark or tape, use sticky-back notes to mark the walls—the newer super-self-sticking notes are ideal, won't fall off the wall over time, and won't damage wallpaper or paint. It also helps to place the fixtures on the floor and outline them. Take care to consider the placement of cabinets when laying out the water supply and drain cleanouts. You may want to temporarily position the cabinets where they will be installed before you complete the supply and drainpipe layouts. When you have completed the layout, measure and adjust the arrangement until all fixtures meet the minimum clearance specifications of the manufacturer and you are comfortable with the layout.

PLACING THE FIXTURES
(minimum allowances)

Make sure a hinged shower door can open completely.

Allow 15" on either side of toilet bowl.

Allow 4" between toilets and sinks and 2" between sinks and tubs.

ROUGH-IN DIMENSIONS

Once your plans are ready, cut holes in your walls and floors for installing drain lines and supply stubs—the supply lines that stick out a bit from the wall and are ready to accept stop valves.

Patching walls and floors can be more time-consuming than the plumbing itself. Where possible, limit your cuts to areas that the fixtures will cover. Cut drywall or plaster neatly so you can patch it easily. Don't forget to install venting (see pages 115–116 and 126–127).

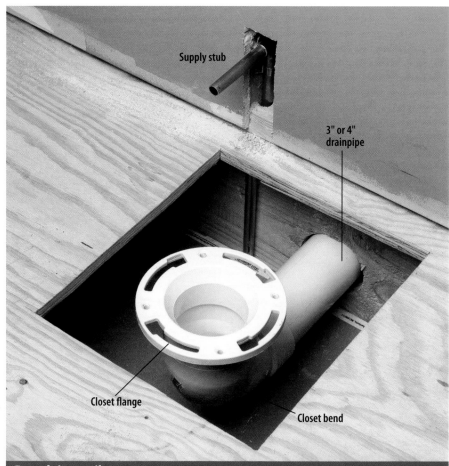

Supply stub

3" or 4" drainpipe

Closet flange

Closet bend

Rough in a toilet

Supply stub   Trap adapter   Supply stub

1½" or 1¼" drainpipe

Rough in a sink

If you are installing a vanity cabinet, you have latitude for placing the drain and supply stubs. For a wall-hung sink or a pedestal sink, hold the fixture up against the wall and mark the best locations for drain and supply stubs (see page 132). In most cases, it is best to position the supply stubs within 12 inches of the faucet.

Be careful to place the closet bend the correct distance from the wall—usually 12 inches to the center of the drain. (Double-check the requirements for your toilet.) You'll place a closet flange on top of the floor after you have patched and surfaced it. Only a cold water supply stub is needed. Place it 6 inches above the floor and to the left of the drainpipe.

FINDING DRAINPIPES

In order to rough in your new drains, you need to know where the existing drain is. Start in the basement or crawlspace. If you see a 3- or 4-inch stack, it probably runs straight through the roof. If not, look for a plumbing access panel. You may find it on the wall opposite your bathroom fixtures. (Often it's in a closet.) Remove the access panel and peer inside with a flashlight.

If you notice a wall is thicker than the standard 4½ inches, it probably contains drainpipes. Toilets usually are placed near stacks.

DRAINAGE DYNAMICS

Plan new drainpipes in walls so they slope toward the branch or main drain stack. A fall of ¼ inch for every foot is best.

When a fixture is farther than 3 feet away from a stack, connect it to a vent pipe that joins a stack or exits through the roof. Check your local building codes for requirements.

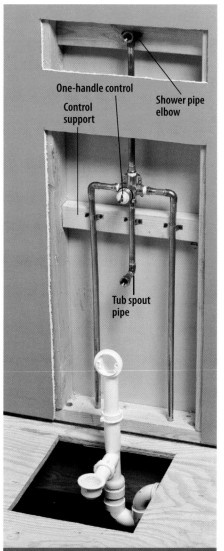

One-handle control
Control support
Shower pipe elbow
Tub spout pipe

Two-handle control
Overflow pipe
Drain assembly

Rough in a shower

To correctly position the drain, set the base in place and measure from the walls. Allow for wall surfacing (see pages 133–134). To spare patching later, cut the floor so the base will cover the hole. Install a P-trap below the level of the floor, at the level the drain assembly kit requires. Install the control assembly. Its size determines how far apart the supply pipes must be. Firmly attach the shower pipe to framing.

Rough in a tub and shower

Cut the floor so the tub will cover the hole. Install a P-trap and bathtub drain assembly. It will be somewhat unstable until you connect it to the tub. The one-handle control shown requires that you plumb the supply lines horizontally into it. Attach the control and the elbow at the top of the shower pipe firmly to framing; you will probably need to frame in a piece of lumber between the studs.

Rough in a two-handle control

A two-handle control is easier to install. Set the hot and cold pipes at the same height. Attach the control or the pipes and the elbow at the top of the shower pipe to frame supports.

CAUTION

BE KIND TO YOUR JOISTS
Don't weaken joists. Deep notches greatly reduce the strength of joists. Drill holes if possible, or reinforce joists after notching.

STAY GROUNDED

Install a jumper wire and ground clamps when you install plastic pipe that separates a section of metal pipe. Many homes use metal plumbing pipes in the electrical grounding system. Jumper wires keep the grounding system intact and keep your home safe.

Installing a tub and shower riser

- **TIME:** 6 to 8 hours
- **SKILLS:** Carpentry skills, connecting plumbing fixtures, soldering
- **TOOLS:** Tape measure, carpenter's level, propane torch, striker, soldering kit, tubing cutter, hammer, power drill, bits, screwdriver

Installing a tub and shower riser requires both plumbing and carpentry skills. And, if you decide to install a whirlpool tub (see pages 138–139), you'll need basic electric wiring skills as well. Sketch an installation drawing of your layout first, then use the drawing to make a tool and materials list.

If replacing an old riser, check for water damage. Include the removal and replacement of damaged or deteriorated subflooring or studs in your plan.

Design a new riser to fit the existing riser holes and blocking for an upgraded project. If the installation involves new construction, you'll need to drill riser holes in the subflooring and install blocking.

For a new installation, decide where you want to place the tub. Locate the nearest water supply. Measure and sketch the run from the water supply.

Installing or upgrading a bathroom riser typically requires a permit. Follow the local codes, and ask your residential building inspector what inspection steps need to be taken during the construction process. Call the local building inspector to make an appointment to inspect the work at each point. Have the inspector sign off before you cover up any work.

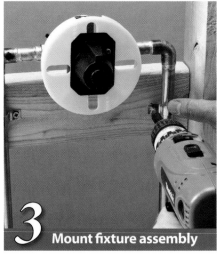

1 Drill for the riser

Determine the best location to tap into supply lines (see pages 122–123). Drill two holes at least ¼ inch larger than the diameter of the riser pipe through the stud wall into the subfloor. The extra permits some flexibility when hooking up the supply lines. The type of fixture you buy determines the distance between the hot and cold supply risers. Refer to the faucet manufacturer's instructions for placement of the risers.

2 Install blocking

Center the tub spout blocking 4 inches above the top of the tub. Install a separate blocking for the faucets, if placing them more than 6 inches above the spout. Make sure that the blocking is level, at the manufacturer's specified depth inside the wall. Toenail it firmly to the studs. The height of the showerhead blocking depends on what suits your needs. The standard height for showerheads is 6 feet 6 inches above the floor.

3 Mount fixture assembly

Measure and record on a drawing the lengths needed for the risers, integral stops, and tub spout. Cut the pieces to the specified lengths. Mount the fixture assembly on the blocking. Make sure it is centered and level. Connect the adapters using joint tape or joint compound.

4 Test-fit pipe run

Assemble the copper tubing and fittings for the riser to test-fit the run. Make sure all the pieces fit. Double-check faucet controls to make sure they're centered and level. Make adjustments before soldering.

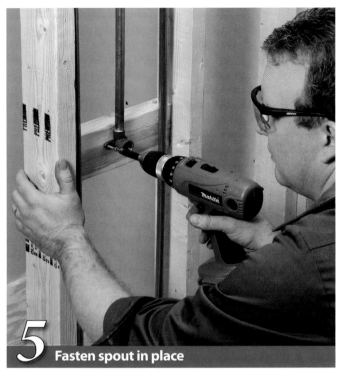

5 Fasten spout in place

Solder the copper fittings (see pages 72–75). Attach the spout.

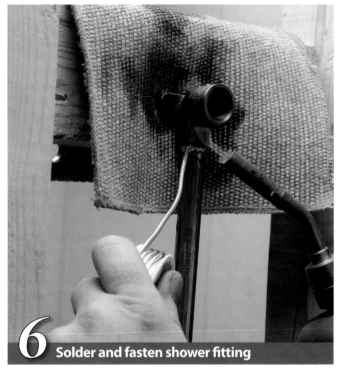

6 Solder and fasten shower fitting

Solder the piping for the showerhead. Secure it to the blocking.

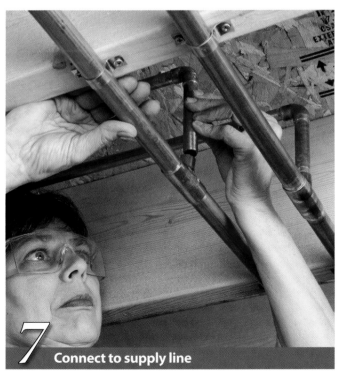

7 Connect to supply line

Before connecting the riser to the supply lines, find out if the inspector wants to have the lines tested. Otherwise connect the supply risers to the supply lines. Turn on the water and check for leaks.

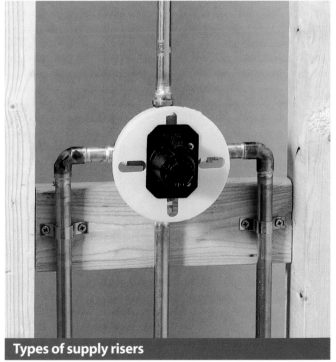

Types of supply risers

Three types of supply risers are available: single-handle, two-handle, and three-handle. Single-handle faucet designs vary among cartridge, ball-type, or disk. The two- and three-handle faucets have either compression or cartridge valves.

Tapping into existing lines

- **TIME:** About 1 day
- **SKILLS:** Joining copper or plastic pipe, basic carpentry skills
- **TOOLS:** Keyhole saw, utility knife, tubing cutter, fine-tooth saw, miter box, groove-joint pliers, hacksaw or reciprocating saw, ratchet with socket, propane torch

When you add a sink close to or on the other side of a wet wall—the wall that contains working plumbing lines—you can tie into existing copper supplies and plastic drain lines. (For tapping into cast-iron pipes, see page 125.) If you have trouble locating the drain line, see the tips on page 118.

Tapping into a wet wall is much easier than installing new drain, vent, and supply lines, but it is still a major project. Don't spoil the job by getting an important detail wrong: A telltale sign of an unprofessional plumbing job is revealed when the hot and cold faucets end up on the wrong sides of the sink. Be sure the hot handle is on the left.

CAUTION

OUT OF ORDER

Tell family members not to use toilets positioned above the place where you have cut the stack, or you will receive an extremely rude surprise.

Also, be aware that sewer gases can escape from an opened stack. Cap the lines with duct tape or stuff rags in them if they will be left open for more than a few minutes.

HELPFUL HINTS

- Don't overnotch. Although the situation is not as critical for walls as it is for floors (see page 119), it is important to preserve the studs' strength; notch as little as you can when making space for pipes.
- Protect pipes from nail punctures. To eliminate any possibility of poking a hole in a pipe when you nail the drywall, protect drainpipes with metal plates placed over notches. If you can, run supply pipes through holes drilled in the centers of studs, out of reach of drywall nails or screws.

1 Anchor the drain line

Shut off the water and drain the lines. Open up the wet wall to the center of the studs on either side of the stack so you will have a nailing surface for patching later. You may have to make a separate hole for access to the supply pipes. To anchor the stack, attach riser clamps above and below the area you will cut.

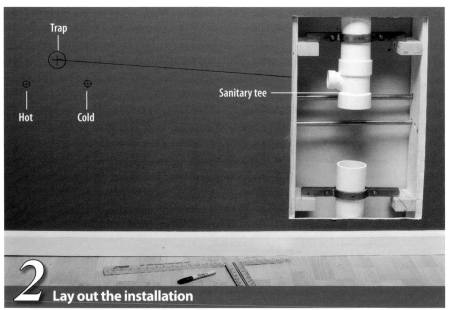

2 Lay out the installation

Plan out the fixture's rough-in dimensions (see page 117) and mark them on the wall. Be sure the location doesn't exceed the maximum distance local codes permit. To determine the point at which the fixture will tie into the stack, draw a line that slopes from the center of the drain trap at ¼ inch per foot. Being careful to cut squarely, use a hacksaw or reciprocating saw to remove a section of stack 8 inches longer than the sanitary tee you'll install.

3 Install the sanitary tee

In most cases, you'll need a sanitary tee to accept 1½-inch pipe; for bathroom sinks, 1¼-inch is sometimes acceptable. Dry-fit the tee, two spacers, and two slip couplings into place as shown. Don't cement them until the rest of the run is completed. Slide the couplings up and down to secure the spacers.

Protective metal plates

Trap adapter 90-degree elbow

4 Install the drainpipe

Cut out a strip of drywall and notch the studs just deep enough to support the pipes. Use a 45-degree elbow and a short spacer at the stack, and a 90-degree elbow and a trap adapter at the trap. Once you're sure the pipe slopes at ¼ inch per foot, scribe all the pieces with alignment marks, then disassemble, prime, and cement the drainpipe pieces together (see pages 82–85).

5 Install supply tees

Tap into copper or plastic supply lines using spacers, slip couplings, and tees similar to those used on the drainpipe. (For soldering copper joints, see pages 72–75.) If you tap into galvanized steel supply lines, you may have to cut and remove sections of pipe and install union connectors. Be sure to use a transition fitting if you're mixing pipe materials, such as copper and iron (see pages 68–69).

Rag to seal off sewer gas

Caps to seal supply lines temporarily

6 Run and cap supply lines

Run pipes to the fixture location using 90-degree elbows and pipe as needed. Use 90-degree elbows and short pieces to bring the lines out past the wall surface. Stuff a rag in the drain to seal off sewer gas. Solder caps on the ends of the supply lines, turn on the water, and test for leaks. Close up the wall, add stop valves (see page 90), and you're ready to install the fixture.

Adding plastic drain lines

Cutting, moving, and refitting plastic pipe are all simple jobs—as long as you have a plastic waste stack and easy access to the drainpipe.

Every drain line must be properly vented (see pages 115–116). Be sure you have this planned before you cut into the drainpipe. You may need to tap in at a second, higher point for the vent.

TIME: If you have easy access to the existing drain, assume a half day for this assembly

SKILLS: Cutting pipe, measuring, aligning, and cementing plastic pipe

TOOLS: Hacksaw or fine-tooth saw, marker, utility knife, drill with hole saw bit or reciprocating saw

CAUTION

PROTECT YOUR EYES

This is a job in which plenty of dirt, burrs, and sawdust will fall from above. Wear goggles when working above your head.

1 Cut out a section of pipe

Measure the new sanitary tee to see how much of the old pipe you need to remove. Take into account the depth of the sockets (see pages 70–71). Be sure that both sides of the existing pipe are supported, so they'll stay in position after the cut is made. Cut with a hacksaw or fine-tooth saw and remove burrs with a utility knife.

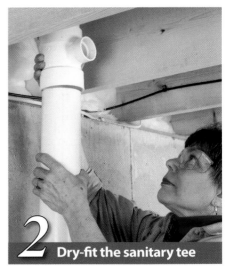

2 Dry-fit the sanitary tee

Install the top end first, then the bottom. You may have to loosen one of your support straps somewhere to give yourself enough play in the pipes to do this. Once the sanitary tee is in the desired position, make an alignment mark with a marker.

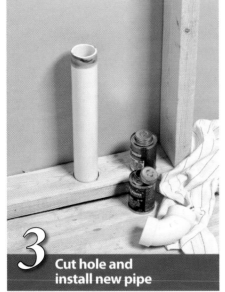

3 Cut hole and install new pipe

Run pipes to the location of the new fixture. If you need to run the drainpipe through wall plates or framing, cut holes to accommodate the pipe. Leave at least ⅝ inch of wood on any side that will receive drywall. This way, nails or screws driven through drywall and into the plate won't pierce the pipe.

4 Connect the pieces

Connect the new drainpipe to the sanitary tee with elbows and lengths of pipe. Dry-fit the pieces, draw alignment lines, disassemble, prime, and cement the pieces together (see pages 82–85). Support the run with at least one strap for the horizontal run.

Tapping into cast-iron drain lines

- **TIME:** Set aside a full day, so you can take your time on this difficult project
- **SKILLS:** Joining plastic pipe and basic carpentry skills
- **TOOLS:** Cast-iron pipe cutter (rent this tool), socket and ratchet, screwdriver, hacksaw or fine-tooth saw

Cast-iron pipe was commonly used for the drain-waste-vent system in older homes. Often one or two large stacks are made of cast iron and the lines leading into them are galvanized steel.

Cast iron is difficult to work with (see Caution below) and it is no longer required for new installations. However, you may need to run a new drain into an existing cast-iron stack. Most likely, you will have to tap in at two places: one for the drain and one for the vent.

This page shows how to break into a cast-iron stack to replace a cast-iron Y-fitting with a plastic sanitary tee. You'll use the same techniques to install a sanitary tee, as shown on page 124.

CAUTION

CONSIDER HIRING A PRO

Working with cast iron is difficult and can be dangerous. Cast iron is heavy, is prone to shattering, and has sharp edges. This is a project that you may want to leave to a professional. Some plumbers will make the cast-iron connections only, allowing you to save money by making the plastic connections yourself.

1 Support the stack

Securely support the stack from above and make sure it is well supported below. (You do not need to move either portion of the cast-iron pipe in order to make the connection.) Use riser clamps specially made for support.

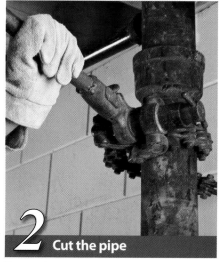

2 Cut the pipe

Rent a chain-type cast-iron pipe cutter. Wrap the chain around the stack and hook it. Then, with the handles open, crank the chain tight with the turn screw. Draw the handles together. This part of the job takes muscle, but if you follow the tool manufacturer's directions, you will get a clean cut.

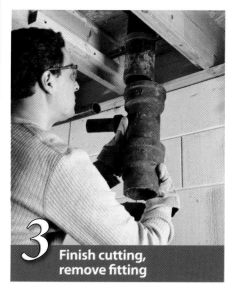

3 Finish cutting, remove fitting

If you are removing a fitting, make a second cut about 4 inches below the first cut, and cut the horizontal run. If the horizontal pipe is galvanized steel, cut it with a hacksaw. Remove the 4-inch section and pull out the fitting.

4 Install no-hub fittings

Install new plastic fittings with no-hub connectors. You may have to use short sections of pipe as spacers. To assemble a no-hub connector, slip the connector over the end of the old pipe, insert the sanitary tee with spacers in place, slide the connector so it bridges the old pipe and the spacers, and install clamps. Tighten clamps with a screwdriver.

Adding new vents

- **TIME:** If there are no major obstructions, count on spending a day running the vent and a day patching the walls
- **SKILLS:** Basic plumbing and carpentry skills
- **TOOLS:** Drill with hole saw bit, knife, keyhole saw, jigsaw or reciprocating saw

If your new fixture is located far from an existing stack, codes may require a new vent. Though you'll have to run the new vent all the way through the roof, doing so may be easier than tying into the existing stack. You'll create less work adding a new stack than you would by reventing and patching, especially if your wall is void of insulation and fire blocking. If you have attic space with exposed pipes, consider running the new vent straight up through the attic. You can tie into the existing vent there. Unlike drainpipes, vent pipes can run horizontally since gases are drawn upward through the vent by the lower atmospheric pressure outside the house.

Calculating drain and vent size for shared fixtures can be daunting. Each fixture added to the system has a unit rating, which is a measure of the peak flow of discharge through a drainpipe. For example, a unit rating of a typical bathroom sink is 7½ gallons per minute. To accurately determine the vent size, you will need to add together the ratings of each fixture that shares a common drain or vent. Fortunately you can save yourself the time of calculating vent size, because the typical bathroom with a toilet, sink, and combination shower and bathtub can be adequately served with a 2-inch vent. Local codes vary, so check with your building inspector for vent size. If you're not installing a toilet, a bathroom sink and bathtub can share a 1½-inch vent.

1 Cut hole for vent pipe

Hole saw bit

In the attic, find the top plate of the wall where the new vent is needed. Choose a spot between two studs and drill through the plate. Size the hole so it's just big enough to accommodate the outside diameter of the pipe.

2 Install roof vent

Mark the point directly above the hole and drive a nail up through the roof. Remove a shingle; cut a hole with a jigsaw or reciprocating saw. (You may need to cut a larger hole if you're increasing pipe size. See Step 4.) If a rafter is in the way, offset the vent with 45-degree elbows.

3 Install the pipe

With a helper, slide a pipe through the holes. Start at the attic and push down. After everything is dry-fitted, prime and cement the joints. Allow for about 2 feet of pipe to extend above the roof—you can trim it as soon as the cement has set and you have checked the fit of the flashing.

Reducer fitting

Vent pipes usually extend 1' above roof

Vent flashing

Larger size pipe may be required

4 Install roof flashing

Secure the vent with a riser clamp (see page 122) in the attic. In cold climates, codes call for an increased pipe size where the pipe pierces the roof. This prevents freeze-ups from clogging the vent. Slip the flashing over the vent; tuck it under the shingles uphill from the vent. Seal with roofing cement.

5 Reventing

If your new fixture is close enough to an existing stack, it is often easiest to revent. However, as the photo shows, this usually requires a major wall-patching job afterward. If the new fittings must be installed in an old cast-iron stack, you will have to go through the steps on page 125.

Running the supply lines

■ **TIME:** About 4 hours to tap into lines and run eight pieces of pipe and their fittings
■ **SKILLS:** Measuring, cutting, and soldering copper pipe
■ **TOOLS:** Hacksaw or tubing cutter, propane torch, groove-joint pliers, adjustable wrench

Once the DWV system is installed, you can tackle the easier job of extending supply lines to the new location. If you are tying into old galvanized pipe, look for a convenient union fitting, open it, and dismantle back to the nearest fittings. Otherwise, tee in the supply by cutting a supply pipe and removing both ends (see page 123). Now you are ready to connect new to old. Turn the water off and drain the lines before cutting pipe or opening unions.

MAINTAINING PRESSURE WHEN ADDING LINES

If the pipes will supply more than two fixtures, use ³⁄₄-inch rather than ¹⁄₂-inch pipe.

If you have a long run (more than 25 feet), use ³⁄₄-inch pipe. Usually it is best to run ³⁄₄-inch pipe into a bathroom, then run ¹⁄₂-inch pipe to each fixture.

Don't move up from ¹⁄₂-inch to ³⁄₄-inch pipe in a line. Step down in dimension, never up.

If you have more than four right-angle bends, make some of them using 45-degree elbows. Too many sharp turns reduce water pressure.

1 Tap in with an adapter

To go from galvanized to copper or plastic (make sure your locality permits the use of plastic supplies if you choose this option), use a dielectric adapter like the one shown here. Never hook copper pipe directly to galvanized pipe—electrolytic action will corrode the connection.

2 Make new pipe connections

Replace the run with copper or plastic pipe and a tee fitting. Splice with a slip coupling and spacer. Solder or cement the pipes and fittings (see page 72–75 and 82–86). As you install the pipes that lead to the new service, slope the lines slightly so you can easily drain the system.

3 Install drop ells

At the new fixture, use drop ells instead of regular elbows. Attach them with screws to a piece of wood that is firmly anchored to the framing. Make sure they are positioned 6 to 8 inches apart.

Run lines to the fittings. Follow the directions given on pages 72–75 for soldering copper pipes, or see pages 82–85 for cementing plastic pipe, or page 86 for PEX pipe. Before soldering copper, open every faucet on the run. Otherwise, heat from the torch can burn out washers and other parts, and built-up steam can rupture a fitting or pipe wall.

Cap the lines, turn on the water, and check for leaks. Don't cover the opening yet; the inspector will want to look at the pipes before you patch the wall.

Installing a hose bib

The task of replacing an existing hose bib faucet with a freezeproof model or installing a new hose bib at a convenient location is a straightforward job. Select a faucet that's long enough to reach well inside the heated house. Install it with a slight downward pitch toward the outside of the house so the pipe drains after the valve is turned off.

Even a freezeproof faucet will freeze and rupture if a hose is left attached. An outdoor faucet remains the most vulnerable element to freezing in your plumbing system. Remove hoses before the first frost. As the temperature falls below 32°F, the water in an exposed pipe freezes, expands, and ruptures the pipe. Ask any homeowner who has had to deal with one: A burst water pipe creates a costly mess.

This project assumes your house is plumbed with copper pipe. If you have galvanized steel pipes, install a dielectric union if you plan to connect copper pipe to the system.

- **TIME:** About 4 hours
- **SKILLS:** Drilling a clean hole, soldering copper pipe, connecting fittings
- **TOOLS:** Tape measure, power drill, spade bit, hole saw, screwdriver, adjustable wrench, groove-joint pliers, pipe flux, lead-free solder, propane torch, emery cloth, tubing cutter, joint tape

1 Drain and cut the supply pipe

Drill a hole through the house using a hole saw. The hole will need to be large enough for the hose bib shaft. From the outside, insert the shaft. Inside the house, locate and mark where you will be tapping into the existing supply line.

Turn off the main water supply valve nearest to the installation or replacement faucet. Drain the line at the main supply valve or a faucet lower than the elevation of the new faucet. The supply line must be completely drained of water and dry before you solder new copper connections. Remove aerators on faucets along the drained line.

Cut the copper pipe at the mark with a mini hacksaw or tubing cutter. Remove any burrs and clean the pipe.

2 Solder the copper pipe

Solder a copper tee and any pipe necessary to install the hose bib stub (see pages 72–75). Solder a threaded adapter fitting to the copper pipe.

CAUTION

WATCH THE FLAME
This job requires soldering with a propane torch. Wear eye protection and protect combustible materials with fire-resistant cloth or sheet metal. As a precaution, keep a fire extinguisher nearby.

3 Install the faucet

Install a union between the adapter and the hose bib shaft. A union makes it easier to remove and replace the hose bib if it becomes damaged. It also means you don't have to turn the hose bib with a wrench to install it, which could damage it. Wrap all threaded fittings with joint tape (see page 81).

On the outside, drive screws through the mounting holes to secure the flange. Caulk around the flange to prevent cold air or pests from entering the house. Close the hose bib faucet valve. Close the drain cap, if open. Turn on the main supply and inspect for leaks. If you have removed faucet aerators, replace them after you flush the lines.

Installing a rimmed sink

- **TIME:** Half a day to cut a hole in the vanity top, install the sink, and hook up the faucet and drain
- **SKILLS:** Basic plumbing and carpentry skills
- **TOOLS:** Jigsaw and extra blades, screwdriver, groove-joint pliers

Setting a new sink in place is one of the truly satisfying plumbing tasks. It signals the completion of a fairly easy job that gets noticed immediately.

When shopping for a new rimmed (also known as deck-mounted) fixture, you'll find plenty of options—stainless steel, cast iron, plastic composite, vitreous china, and more. Most kitchen and bath sinks manufactured today are self-rimming, which means installation is as easy as putting some putty on the rim and clamping the sink to the countertop.

To remove an old sink, turn off the supply stops or shut off the water to your house and drain the lines. Disconnect the supply lines and the trap that joins the sink to the drainpipe. Remove mounting clips from underneath and pry up the sink.

1 **For a bathroom sink, first cut an opening**

If you need to cut a hole for the sink, trace the template provided with the sink onto the countertop surface. Drill an entry hole and cut the opening using a jigsaw and fine-tooth blade.

2 **Attach fixtures**

Before lowering the sink into the opening, hook up the faucet (see pages 92–94) and drain assembly (see page 60). With bathroom sinks, the drain assembly consists of a basin outlet flange, drain body, gasket, locknut, and tailpiece, which slides into the P-trap. (Installing these after you install the sink is difficult, and you also risk damaging the parts.) Lay a bead of plumber's putty around the basin outlet, insert the flange, and screw together the other parts of the drain assembly.

3 **Set the sink**

Apply a thick bead of silicone adhesive around the underside of the fixture's flange, about ¼ inch from the edge. Turn the sink right side up and lower it carefully into the opening. Press down on the sink; some of the caulk will ooze out. Wipe away the excess. After the silicone adhesive has set (about two hours), apply latex caulk around the sink.

Installing stainless-steel sinks

Do not cut this line; cut 1" or so inside it

1 For a stainless-steel sink, mark and cut an opening

Turn your sink upside down on the countertop. Make sure it is in the correct position, safely set back from the cabinet beneath. Trace the outline of the sink, then draw a line that is an inch or so to the inside of that outline. Erase the first line to make sure you do not cut it. Cut the opening using a circular saw with a fine-tooth blade for the straight cuts and a jigsaw for curves. Take your time to make a clean cut. Test the sink for fit.

2 Attach the faucets and strainer

Attach a basket strainer to each bowl. Lay a bead of putty around the outlet, set the gasket in place, and lower the strainer body into the hole. With your other hand, from underneath, slip the friction ring in place, and screw on the locknut. Tighten, and clean away the putty that oozes out. You also can attach the tailpiece and trap assembly at this point. To install the faucet, see pages 92–94.

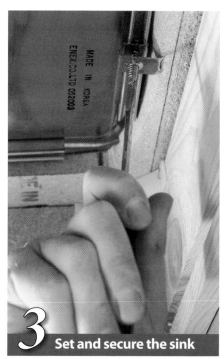

3 Set and secure the sink

To set the sink, first place a rope of plumber's putty all around the rim. Turn the sink right side up and lower it into the opening. Secure the sink to the countertop with sink clips every 6 to 8 inches. Working from underneath the sink, tighten the clips with a screwdriver. Remove excess putty with a putty knife and a rag dipped in paint thinner.

Install a cast-iron sink

To set a cast-iron kitchen sink, use the same technique used to set the rimmed sink. Run a bead of silicone sealant under the rim, turn the sink right side up, set it in place, and wipe away the excess sealant. Run caulk along the edge and smooth it with a finger.

Installing a wall-mount or pedestal sink

- **TIME:** A half day to add framing and install a new sink (not including drywall patching and painting)
- **SKILLS:** Basic plumbing and carpentry skills
- **TOOLS:** Keyhole saw, hammer, level, screwdriver or drill/driver, groove-joint pliers or pipe wrench

Wall-mount bathroom sinks are not as popular as they once were but remain useful where space is limited or a retro style is desired. Installing the bracket support is a time-consuming part of this job. Some wall-mount sinks have legs at the front corners for added support.

A pedestal sink installs like a wall-mount sink and has a decorative pedestal that adds support and hides the drain plumbing.

CAUTION

DON'T SIT ON THE SINK

Bracket-supported sinks stand up to normal everyday use, but warn members of the household not to sit on them. They could crack or pull away from the wall.

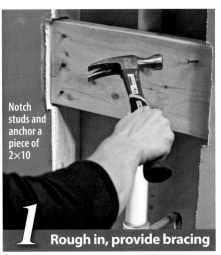

Notch studs and anchor a piece of 2×10

1 Rough in, provide bracing

Shut off the water and drain the line. To remove an old fixture, disconnect the drain and supply lines. Then look underneath to see if it is held by bolts. If so, loosen or cut the bolts. Pull straight up on the sink to dislodge it.

For a new installation, run new supply lines and provide solid framing for the hanger bracket.

Level

Mounting bracket

2 Finish wall, install anchor bracket

Install the drywall. You can tape it and paint now too; it will be easier than after the sink is installed. Secure the wall bracket to the 2×10 blocking using wood screws, not drywall screws. Make sure the bracket is level as you drive in the screws. Install stop valves (see page 90).

3 Set sink in place

Turn the sink on its side and install the faucet and the drain assembly. Attach flexible supply lines to the sink. Hold the sink above the bracket, against the wall, and lower it onto the bracket. A flange fits into a slot in the sink. Have a helper guide the supply tubes into the stop valves.

4 Attach legs or pedestal

If your sink comes with support legs, insert them into the holes in the bottom of the sink, plumb them, and adjust them to firmly support the sink. Most legs adjust by turning the top part of the leg. Test the sink for level. Many pedestals attach to the floor and rest against the underside of the sink. You can caulk the joint.

5 Hook up supplies and drain

Connect the supply lines to the stop valves. Connect the trap to the sink drain and the drainpipe. Turn the water back on and check the supply lines for leaks. Run some water into the bowl with the stopper closed, then open the stopper to check the drain lines for leaks.

Installing a shower surround

- **TIME:** About 2 days; 1 day to install and 1 day to allow the adhesive to dry before use
- **SKILLS:** Carpentry skills, basic plumbing skills, using adhesives
- **TOOLS:** Tape measure, level, utility knife, straightedge, pencil, caulking gun, power drill, carbide hole saw, adjustable wrench

A preformed fiberglass shower enclosure is a convenient alternative to waiting in line to use the shower. Easier and faster than tiling a shower, the process is well within the abilities of the average do-it-yourselfer. If the base and plumbing are already in place, you can complete the shower installation over the weekend.

Measure the space for the shower. You will want to purchase the largest enclosure that will fit the available space. Avoid installing an enclosure that's smaller than a 3-foot square. Elbow room is a necessity, and a shower that is too small will not get used.

Prefabricated enclosures
Fiberglass shower units are an easy alternative compared to the work involved in constructing a tiled shower. Choices vary from very narrow units to spacious enclosures.

Simple elegance
Prefabricated shower stalls are available in a variety of shapes and colors to fit virtually any bathroom style and floor plan.

1 Prepare the walls

Cover the framing with greenboard (moisture-resistant drywall) or cement backerboard. This is particularly important for areas near the enclosure; they will often get wet. Tape, then prime or seal the walls before installing the panels. If you're working in an existing shower area, shut off the water supply and remove any handles. An enclosure can be installed onto wall tiles as long as you clean and rinse them thoroughly, to ensure that the adhesive will stick. Finish cleaning using denatured alcohol.

INSULATE TO REDUCE NOISE

Packing the walls of a shower with insulation reduces the tin-roof sound of water against the thin shower walls.

Installing a shower surround *(continued)*

2 Make a template

First, install the side panel with the plumbing cutouts. To ensure against cutting mistakes—which cannot be corrected—make a template using a large piece of cardboard (the shipping carton is a good source). Measure over from the wall and up from the shower pan to locate the center of each hole and transfer those measurements to the template. Use a compass to draw circles the size of the openings. Cut the template and test it for fit. Correct any mistakes using scrap cardboard pieces and masking tape.

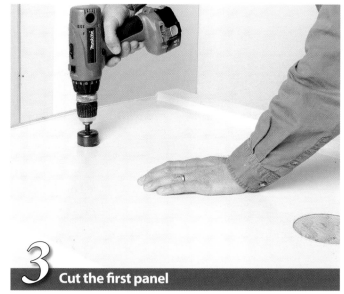

3 Cut the first panel

Lay the panel on a flat surface and place the template on top. Use masking tape to hold the template's edges flush with the panel's edges. Use a pencil or felt-tipped marker to scribe the cutout lines. Drill smaller holes using a hole saw. You may need a jigsaw for a larger hole. The holes should be large enough to accommodate the plumbing, but small enough for the escutcheons (flanges) to completely cover the hole. Test-fit the panel; you may need to trim it.

4 Affix the first panel

Use a caulk gun to apply squiggles of adhesive recommended by the manufacturer to the back of the panel. Apply adhesive to the edges as well as the middle of the panel. Set the panel on the base, align it, then arch it against the wall, gently pressing it into place. Once you are sure it is correctly positioned, press more firmly to transfer some adhesive to the wall. Pull the panel back a few inches and wait a minute or so for the adhesive to begin to set. Press the panel back in place. Once you are sure it is correctly positioned, press and run your hands from side to side as well as up and down until it is firmly attached to the wall at all points.

5 Affix the remaining panels

The remaining panels may not need to be cut. Test each for fit, then adhere them as described in Step 4.

Installing a bathtub

- **TIME:** 4 to 6 hours
- **SKILLS:** Carpentry skills, connecting plumbing fixtures, soldering
- **TOOLS:** Tape measure, carpenter's level, propane torch, striker, soldering kit, tubing cutter, hammer, power drill, bits, screwdriver

The bathtub has become the major focal point in a bathroom design. Before beginning the hunt for the perfect bathtub, take note of your household members' bathing habits. A whirlpool tub might be attractive, but a standard tub-shower combination with accessories such as a seat or multiple showerheads may be a better choice.

Think through the installation before buying the tub and having it delivered. A standard tub measures 60 inches long by 30 inches wide and holds about 50 gallons of water. The benefit of installing a standard-size tub is that it's not too difficult to get into the bathroom or up a flight of stairs.

Luxury soaking tubs and whirlpools require a more creative approach to transport to a second-floor bathroom. Their bulk may make it impossible to negotiate the stairs. You may have to consider pulling out a window or opening a wall to hoist the tub into the bathroom. Stairs can also be a problem if the tub comes with a built-in enclosure. To avoid such problems, buy a multipiece unit.

Tubs without enclosures offer two choices for apron placement: either left-end aprons or right-end aprons. Your choice of which to purchase is based on faucet placement. If you can't decide which one you want, a tub with a reversible apron gives you the flexibility to decide later. Faucets and fittings are always purchased separately.

Half-inch supply pipes make filling an oversize tub a time-consuming task. When installing the control risers and supply line (see pages 120–121), consider installing ¾-inch supply lines.

Also, your old water heater may have served you well in the past, but pair it with a larger tub and the result is tepid bathwater. Keep in mind that tubs with capacities of up to 80 gallons require a 50- to 75-gallon water heater. If a new water heater is not a possibility, purchase a tub that has an in-line heater. These heaters are installed with spa heads so they recirculate bathwater continually, maintaining a consistent temperature.

Most residential bathroom floors are constructed to support the weight of a standard bathtub. Some custom homes will accommodate oversize tubs. Determine whether you need to beef up the floor joists to support an oversize tub or whirlpool.

Removing the old tub

1 Disconnect the drain

Loosen the screws on the overflow plate and remove it. Pull out the trip lever and linkage. Remove the strainer. Unscrew the drain piece with a pair of pliers and a screwdriver. Pull out the stopper with the linkage attached.

2 Cut the wall away

If the existing wall is tiled, chisel into the grout and pry off at least one course of tile along the edge of the tub. Cut away the wall to reveal the tub flange. Remove the screws or nails that fasten the flange to the studs or ledger.

3 Remove the tub

You may be able to pry the tub loose, depending on how it was installed. Pull the tub away from the wall. Have a helper assist you with removing and disposing of it. You may have to cut it up or break it to remove it.

Installing a bathtub *(continued)*

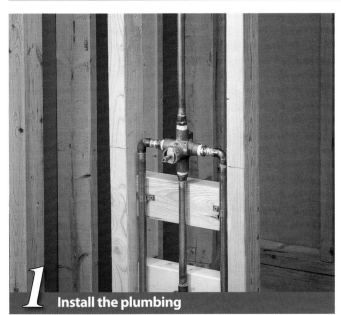

1 Install the plumbing

If you need to frame new walls for the tub, frame them so the alcove opening is just large enough to slide the tub into place. Leave a gap of ⅛ inch or less at the head and foot of the tub. Install plumbing for the risers, faucet, and showerhead (see pages 120–121). Make sure you install an access panel so you can get to the valves in case of an emergency.

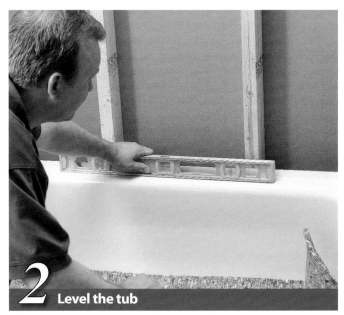

2 Level the tub

Slide the tub into the alcove to test-fit. Set some old blankets or towels, or the shipping cardboard, over the tub floor to protect the bottom of the tub. A dropped tool can do major damage to a tub. Check the tub with a carpenter's level. Shim until it is level. Stay away from using wood shims because they rot when exposed to moisture. The best shims are flattened copper tubing or plastic shims. Mark the location of the top of the nailing flange at each stud. Remove the tub.

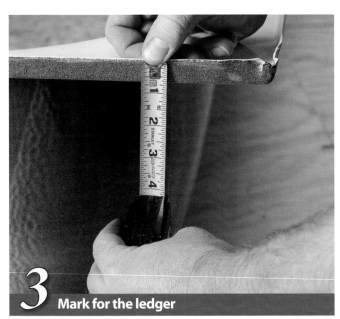

3 Mark for the ledger

The ledger board helps support the tub. You'll need to determine the proper height for it by measuring the depth of the nailing flange. Measure this distance down from the previous mark on each stud and make a second mark. These marks serve as a guide for placing the top ledger board.

4 Install the drainpipes

If the drainpipe and P-trap are not already roughed in, you need to install them. Cut an access hole that extends 10 inches from the center of the end wall in the subfloor (page 117). Connect a 1½-inch P-trap. Install a slip nut fitting centered directly under the overflow pipe location of the tub.

5 Install the ledger board

Cut the ledger boards and drive wood screws or galvanized nails to attach them to the wall studs at the marks you made earlier. Some tubs require additional support braces; you may need to adjust the ledger board lengths. Check the ledger boards for level before installing the tub.

6 Connect the overflow

Trim the drainpipe as specified in the tub manufacturer's instructions so it will fit the overflow kit. The drainpipe should seat snugly into the pressure fitting on the P-trap. You may have to trim the pipe so it fits. Connect the overflow and drain to the tub. Follow the manufacturer's instructions for connecting the drain and overflow assembly on the tub.

7 Install the tub

Position the tub on the ledgers. The tub must sit firmly against the ledger boards, and the tub drain must fit snugly into the P-trap. Drive galvanized nails into the studs through the predrilled holes in the tub flange. If there are no predrilled holes, anchor the tub to the studs with the nailheads as shown.

8 Insert the drain linkage

Snake the drain linkage through the overflow opening. Attach the overflow cover plate and the drain assembly. Test the system for leaks. Before you finish the walls and installation, schedule an inspection. Don't enclose walls prior to inspection, or you may be required to tear out some of your work.

9 Complete the installation

Finish the tub walls. Install the fixtures. Seal around the faucet handles and tub spout with a good-quality tub-and-tile caulk. Apply a bead of caulk around the edge of the tub. Use your finger to smooth the caulk. Turn on the water and check for leaks. Wait at least 24 hours before using the tub to allow caulking to dry.

Installing a whirlpool tub

■ **TIME:** 6 to 8 hours
■ **SKILLS:** Carpentry skills, connecting plumbing fixtures, soldering
■ **TOOLS:** Tape measure, carpenter's level, propane torch, striker, soldering kit, tubing cutter, hammer, power drill, bits, screwdriver, carpentry tools for custom surround

A t a home center or specialty store, you can find a wide variety of whirlpools (also called spas). If you choose the right model and plan carefully, installing a whirlpool is within the capabilities of a do-it-yourselfer.

Choosing a whirlpool

Many large units with molded fiberglass sides and a deck can be installed almost as quickly as a standard tub, since they require little framing and no tiling. Some smaller whirlpools are designed to fit in the same space as a standard tub (though they are typically wider). A drop-in model, as shown on these pages, calls for more planning and work, but it allows you to be creative in designing the surrounding space.

Some models come with their own spout and handles. This eases the installation quite a bit.

Choose a unit that has an integral heating unit, to keep the water hot for as long as you want.

If you'd like to install a large whirlpool, make sure that it will fit through your doors. Some models are so large that they can be installed only in new construction, before the walls are completely framed.

If you will use the whirlpool only as a soaking tub, you need only a tub spout, and a shower door is strictly optional. Most whirlpools can be used as showers, but you must install a shower faucet and a door or a curtain.

Cutting the opening

Frame the walls out of 2×4s and cut a plywood deck to fit. Use a cardboard template (which may be supplied by the manufacturer) to mark for cutting the hole. Also drill holes for the handles and the spout.

TUB INSTALLATION MISTAKES

Avoid the mistakes that commonly occur during tub installation:
- Violating or ignoring local code restrictions regarding drain and supply lines, as well as the electrical receptacle.
- Undersizing the pipes.
- Attaching copper to galvanized without a brass or dielectric fitting.
- Failing to wrap pipes with joint tape or apply pipe compound at threaded joints.
- Failing to level the whirlpool.

Installation considerations

Read the manufacturer's literature before you purchase a whirlpool, to learn the installation requirements.

Plumbing a whirlpool is often not much more complicated than plumbing a standard tub. With most units, you need to supply only one hot and one cold water line, plus a drain. The whirlpool comes with supply tubes for the jets already installed.

The drain line must be positioned accurately, so you can make the connection with the tub while reaching into the space from outside. Depending on the design, the spout and control handles may be run through knockout holes in the whirlpool itself, on the surrounding deck, or on the wall.

You will need to provide a code-approved electrical receptacle at the proper location. In most cases, the receptacle must be GFCI-protected. The receptacle should be accessible after the tub is installed.

The plumbing should be accessible as well. As with a standard tub, you should install access panels so you can reach the drain line and the shutoff valves. You also must provide access to the whirlpool's working parts—especially the pump—to make possible future maintenance and repairs.

Because whirlpool tubs are usually made of flexible fiberglass or acrylic, many manufacturers recommend setting the tub in a bed of wet mortar. The mortar firms the floor of the whirlpool, so it won't flex when you stand on it. Excessive flexing can crack the bottom of the tub and cause leaks.

Installing a custom surround

With the whirlpool on-site so you can check dimensions as you work, build the framing for the surround. Take into account the thickness of the backerboard and tiles that will be installed onto the framing. Also keep in mind that the bottom of the tub should rest on a bed of mortar, which raises it up an inch or so.

Build the frame out of 2x4s, then add a plywood deck. Cut out a hole for the whirlpool, and test that it fits. Remove the tub and run the plumbing lines. Test-fit the whirlpool again to make sure that the drain lines up.

Pour a mortar bed onto the subfloor, set the whirlpool in place, and connect the drain. Once the mortar has set, tile the surround and install the spout and the handles.

Getting the fit right

In most cases, the whirlpool's lip should be supported all around the perimeter of the tub, and the bottom should rest in a bed of mortar. Use temporary spacers to keep the lip raised slightly, so you can slip tiles under it.

Installing an antiscald device

Antiscald devices are an important feature to consider if you have small children in your household. Hot tap water accounts for a quarter of the scald burns that require hospitalization among children 4 years and under. Small children do not perceive danger, have less control of their environment, and have a limited ability to react.

Antiscald devices help prevent these situations by regulating water temperature. Many communities have local codes that require new construction to install devices that maintain water temperatures at or below 120°F and prevent sudden changes in water temperature.

You can install these devices yourself. However, if you're considering installing a whole-house device, it's recommended that you hire a professional.

Water safety

If you have small children in your home, you need to consider using antiscald devices for all faucets and showerheads.

KEEP YOUR FAMILY SAFE

- Never leave a small child alone in a bathroom or kitchen. Take the child with you if you must leave the room.
- Set the water heater thermostat to 120°F or less. The lower the setting, the lower the risk of scalds or burns from hot water.
- Install antiscald devices on bathtub faucets and showerheads.
- Always check the water temperature before placing a child in the bathtub or shower. Hold your whole hand in the water and spread your fingers wide. Move your hand back and forth through the water for several seconds, checking for hot spots or surges.

Glossary

For words not listed here, or for more about those that are, refer to the index (pages 142–143)

ABS (acrylonitrile-butadiene-styrene). A rigid black plastic pipe used predominantly for drain-waste-vent (DWV) systems.

Access panel. A removable panel in a wall or ceiling that permits repair or replacement of concealed components.

Adapter. A fitting that facilitates connection of unlike pieces. Transition adapters join different kinds of pipe. Trap adapters connect drain lines to sink traps.

Aerator. A device screwed into the spout outlet of most sink faucets that mixes air with the water to achieve less water splash and smoother flow.

Air chamber. A short, enclosed tube on a water line that provides a cushion of air to absorb shock when flow stops quickly. See *water-hammer arrestor*.

Air gap. A device that prevents drain water from siphoning into supply lines. Check local codes.

Auger. A flexible metal cable to dislodge obstructions in drain lines.

Ballcock. A float valve assembly that regulates water flow into a toilet tank.

Ball valve. A valve using a ball to seal against the seat.

Basin wrench. A wrench with swivel jaws attached to a long handle used to reach tailpiece nuts that are difficult to reach with a normal wrench.

Blow bag. A rubber bladder with a hose fitting on one end and a nozzle on the other. When water is introduced with a hose, it expands tightly in the pipe and releases pulsating bursts of water using the force of the water to clear line blockages.

Check valve. A valve that allows flow in only one direction to prevent backflow.

Cleanout. A removable plug in a trap or a drainpipe that allows easier access to clear blockages inside.

Closet bend. The elbow-shaped fitting beneath toilets that carries waste to the main drain.

Compression fitting. A connection in which a nut compresses a sleeve or ferrule onto copper or plastic tube to form a sealed joint.

Coupling. A fitting used to connect two lengths of pipe in a straight run.

Dielectric union. A fitting to join copper and steel pipe, preventing a corrosive chemical reaction.

Drain-waste-vent (DWV) system. The pipes and fittings that carry liquid and solid wastes out of a building to a public sewer, septic tank, or cesspool. It also allows for the passage of sewer gases to the outside.

Drum trap. A canister trap used in sewer lines of older homes, typically constructed of lead or cast iron.

Elbow. A fitting that changes the direction of a line. Also known as an ell. Called "bends" in drain-waste-vent lines.

Fall. The slope at which drain lines are installed to ensure proper drainage. Minimum fall per foot is ¼ inch.

Fitting. Any connector (except a valve) that joins pipes of similar or dissimilar size or material in a straight run or at an angle.

Fixture drain. The drainpipe and trap leading from a fixture to the main drain.

Flapper. The part of a flush valve that seals the water into the tank when closed or allows the water to exit when opened during the flush cycle.

Float ball. The ball connected to the ballcock inside the toilet tank.

Flux. A rosin applied to the surfaces of copper and brass pipes and fittings before soldering to clean them.

Grease trap. A trap that captures grease entering the drainpipe before it reaches the sewer. This type of trap requires periodic cleaning.

Hose bib. A faucet with an outlet threaded for a garden hose.

Increaser. A fitting used to enlarge a vent stack as it passes through the roof.

Inside diameter (ID). The measurement across the inside of a pipe.

Joint tape. A synthetic material wrapped around pipe threads to seal a joint. See also pipe joint compound.

Main drain. That portion of the drainage system between the fixture drains and the sewer drain. See also fixture drain and sewer drain.

Nipple. Pipe 12 inches or shorter with threads on both ends. A close nipple has threads that meet at the center.

No-hub pipe. A type of cast-iron pipe joined by fittings and stainless-steel clamps with rubber gaskets.

Nominal size. The designated dimension of a pipe or fitting. It varies slightly from the actual size. See also inside diameter.

O-ring. A round rubber washer used to create a watertight seal.

Outside diameter (OD). The measurement across the end of a pipe on the outside. See also inside diameter and nominal size.

P-trap. See *trap*.

Packing. Material used mainly around faucet stems to form a watertight seal.

PB (polybutylene). A flexible plastic tubing used, where allowed by code, in water supply systems.

Pipe joint compound. A material applied to pipe threads to ensure a watertight seal. Also called pipe dope. See also joint tape.

Plumber's putty. A doughlike material used as a sealant.

Plunger. A tool used to dislodge obstructions from drain lines. Also called a force cup and a plumber's friend.

PSI. An abbreviation for pounds per square inch, a measure of water pressure.

PVC (polyvinyl chloride). A rigid plastic pipe used in drain-waste-vent systems.

Reducer. A fitting that joins a larger pipe to a smaller one.

Relief valve. A device designed to open if it senses excess temperature or pressure.

Riser. Any vertical pipe or assembly.

Rough-in. The stage of a plumbing project in which supply and drain-waste-vent lines are run to their destinations.

Run. Any length of pipe or pipes and fittings going in a straight line.

Saddle tee. A fitting used to tap into a water line without having to break the line apart. Some codes prohibit its use.

Saddle valve. A saddle tee with a valve to supply water to a low-demand appliance such as an icemaker.

Sanitary fitting. Any connector used to join drain-waste-vent lines, designed to direct waste flow downward.

Sanitary sewer. The underground line that carries liquid and solid waste to a treatment plant.

Septic tank. A reservoir that collects and separates liquid and solid waste, diverting the liquid waste onto a drainage field.

Sewer drain. That part of the drainage system that carries liquid and solid waste from a dwelling to a sanitary sewer, septic tank, or cesspool.

Shutoff valve. A valve installed alongside the water meter and on branch lines to shut off the entire system.

Soil stack. A vertical drainpipe that carries waste toward the sewer drain. The main soil stack is the largest vertical drain line of a building into which liquid and solid waste from branch drains flow. See also vent stack.

Soldering. A technique employing a molten metal alloy to produce watertight joints between various types of metal pipes and fittings.

Solvent-welding. A method of making watertight joints between plastic pipes and fittings using a chemical solvent.

Stop valve. A valve in a water supply line, usually near a fixture, that shuts off water to the fixture without interrupting service to the rest of the system.

Tailpiece. Part of a fixture drain that joins the drain outlet and the trap.

Tee. A T-shape fitting used to tap into a length of pipe at a 90-degree angle to begin a branch line.

Thermocouple. A device used in a gas water heater to shut off gas flow if the pilot light goes out. A thermocouple consists of two dissimilar metals joined so that electricity is generated when the joint is heated.

Trap. The pipe bend that creates a water seal to prevent sewer gases from entering a home's interior. Codes require that all fixtures be trapped.

Uniform Plumbing Code (UPC). A nationally recognized set of guidelines prescribing safe plumbing practices. Local codes take precedence over this when the two differ.

Union. A fitting used to join pieces of threaded pipe.

Valve. A device to regulate the flow of water in a supply system or fixture.

Valve seat. The nonmoving part of a valve. The flow of water stops when the stem or movable part of the valve comes in contact with the valve seat.

Vent. The vertical or sloping horizontal portion of a drain line that permits sewer gases to exit the house. Every fixture in a house must be vented.

Vent stack. The upper portion of a vertical drain line through which gases pass directly to the outside. The main vent stack is the portion of the main vertical drain line above the highest fixture connected to it.

Water hammer. A loud noise caused by a sudden stop in the flow of water, which causes pipes to move.

Water-hammer arrestor. A device installed at an appliance or fixture to absorb the hydraulic shock created by a sudden shutoff of water, such as occurs when operating a clothes washer. See *air chamber*.

Index

CONFIDENCE

is the direct result of doing it yourself.

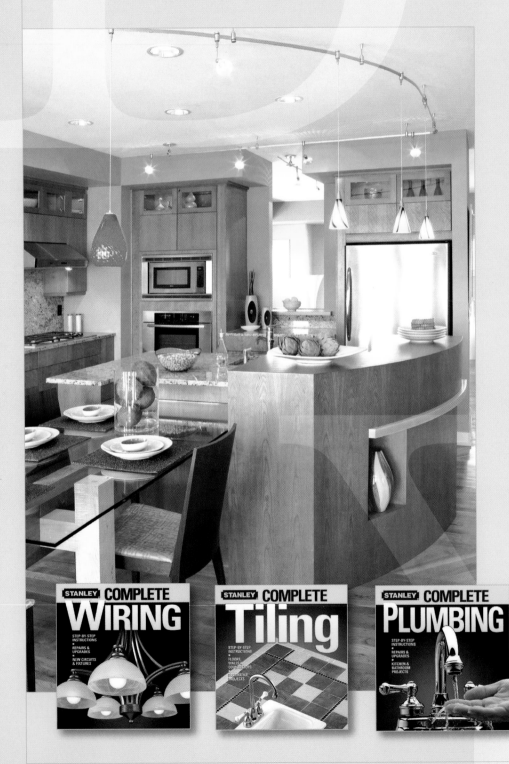

With clear photos, illustrations and easy to follow instructions you'll have the ideas and knowledge to enhance and add value to your home.

LOOK FOR THESE EXCITING HOME IMPROVEMENT TITLES WHEREVER BOOKS ARE SOLD.